Mallarmé and the Sublime

Intersections: A SUNY Series in Philosophy and Literary Criticism

Rodolphe Gasché and Mark C. Taylor, Editors

Mallarmé and the Sublime

Louis Wirth Marvick

State University of New York Press

Published by
State University of New York Press, Albany

Printed in the United States of America

For information, address State University of New York Press, State University Plaza, Albany, N.Y., 12246

Library of Congress Cataloging in Publication Data

Marvick, Louis Wirth, 1954-
Mallarmé and the sublime.

(Intersections: a SUNY series in philosophy and literary criticism)
Bibliography: p. 165
Includes index.
1. Mallarmé, Stéphane, 1842-1898—Criticism and interpretation. 2. Sublime, The, in literature.
I. Title II. Series: Intersections (Albany, N.Y.)
PQ2344.Z5M29 1986 841′.8 85-27750
ISBN 0-88706-278-4
ISBN 0-88706-279-2 (pbk.)

To my parents

Contents

Part Two

Preface

The history of the sublime in modern French and English aesthetic theory has been the subject of numerous articles and at least six book-length studies. Depending on the particular scholarly or polemical aims of their authors, these studies have focused on the place of the sublime in eighteenth-century neoclassical theory; in Gothic fiction and the graveyard school of English poetry; in relation to the philosophy of Kant; in the development of a theory of tragedy in the nineteenth century; or in the vigorous flowering and mannered decay of the Romantic sensibility. As a rule, however, the sublime was not explicitly invoked in defense of any aesthetic position later than about 1820; nor is it nowadays applied in critical discussions of literature produced after that date. The reasons for this are not easy to see—especially since there is so little agreement among scholars about the significance of developments in the evolution of the sublime even *within* the chronological boundaries set for it. Thus Brody claims that Monk has misread Boileau,[1] and Albrecht reproaches him with exaggerating the role of association in Dennis's early treatise on aesthetic experience[2]; yet Monk's work[3] is described as "definitive" by Whalley,[4] who claims another authority "overmodernizes" Longinus; and so on. In short, recent attempts to describe the fortunes of the sublime in the history of taste and assign a correct emphasis to its moral, psychological and aesthetic aspects with the benefit of hindsight have done as much to prolong as to resolve the old controversy. This is a welcome state of affairs, since it suggests that the sublime is not a discardable artifact but a concept which retains its former power to illuminate and confuse. Whalley's observation that, "though not greatly in fashion today, it remains a perennially moving plea for greatness of spirit in literature" attests to the continuing vitality of the sublime; and an investigation of its fortunes subsequent to 1820 is clearly worthwhile.

In recent years, and particularly since his reputation has prospered under the championship of structuralist critics like Gérard Genette and Julia Kristeva, Stéphane Mallarmé has been singled out as the great original of the late nineteenth century, a theorist whose radical proposals concerning the nature of poetry are distinguished from the bloodless "aesthetic" doctrines of his contemporaries by the extent to which they prefigured many of the ideas that have proved most valuable in twentieth-century speculation about the properties and limits of poetic language. But this popularity has emphasized the timelessness of his contribution at the expense of its *relative* novelty in the history of ideas. From the latter point of view, Mallarmé's poetic theories are conspicuous for their resemblance to (and divergence from) the formulations of the sublime advanced by Longinus, Johnson, Burke, Coleridge and others. This connection has not so far been examined in depth—perhaps because of the gulf of ninety years that separates Mallarmé from the thick of the controversy, or because his highly personal vocabulary and difficult prose style obscure the similarity of subject matter. Yet the word "sublime" does appear several times in Mallarmé's prose writings; and at least two critics have referred, in passing, to this quality in his work.[5]

An essay on Mallarmé and the sublime, then, divides itself naturally into two parts. In part one a number of theories of the sublime are examined and a criterion for the sublime sufficiently flexible to allow for the wide discrepancies between them is reached. In part two, Mallarmé's understanding of the term "sublime" is deduced from an analysis of the contexts in which it appears in his prose writings. That understanding is then compared to the criterion evolved in part one, which is applied in turn to the same passages, in order to ascertain whether they illustrate the quality to which they allude. This comparative procedure affords an insight, finally, into the nature both of Mallarmé's literary achievement and of the sublime experience in general.

Two preliminary points remain to be made. First, it must be understood that the scope of this study does not extend to Mallarmé's poetry. Our purpose has rather been to provide, by an analysis of those passages in his writings in which the sublime is explicitly mentioned, a critical tool for an eventual study of the poetry, which, as the volume of exegetical and interpretative literature on that subject suggests, would necessarily be of considerable length in itself.

The second point relates to the argument of part one. We have described each of the theories of the sublime considered therein as the expression of an attitude towards the ideal—an attitude composed in every case of *irony* and *enthusiasm* (in varying proportions). The rhetorical effects produced by the operation of these principles have been the main subject of our study. This approach, moreover, has enabled us to expand in some degree upon Kant's model of the sublime moment, which we saw to be validated, in its basic design, by the effect of the passages examined in chapters ten and twelve. The temptation arising from this choice of central terms to refer to the subjective aspect of the sublime experience rather than to its objective structure, has been resisted throughout.

I wish to thank Professors Michael Riffaterre, Eric Gans, Nathan Leites and Michael Gelven for their criticism and advice. My greatest debt is to my brother Andrew Marvick, without whose encouragement the work might not have been completed.

Part One

Chapter One

Objections to the topic. Limitations of an historical approach. The proper application of the word "sublime" traditionally disputed. An indefinable term?

It is best to meet the objections which might be made to the argument of the present study at once, in order to dispel the suggestion of gratuitousness which automatically attaches to a comparison as unlikely as the one proposed. If Mallarmé had made frequent reference to some aspect or representative of the sublime tradition, this preliminary defense of the comparison might be omitted; but he did not; and as the subject of a contribution to intellectual history it should be skeptically considered. Whatever justification of itself the topic may prove to contain will emerge more clearly after its weaknesses have been acknowledged. Moreover, as J. S. Mill observed, the advocate of a position "must know [his adversary's arguments] in their most plausible and persuasive form; he must feel the whole force of the difficulty which the true view of the subject has to encounter and dispose of, else he will never really possess himself of the portion of truth which meets and removes that difficulty."[1]

The devil's advocate in this case would base his indictment on two points: first, that the sublime has been so variously and contradictorily defined as to render the demonstration of an affinity between Mallarmé and one of its proponents tantamount to the demonstration of his hostility towards another; and second, that, even granted the possibility of distinguishing some constant set of sublime attributes in the welter of definitions, a number of elements in Mallarmé's poetry will still be found not to assort with them. To this might be added the charge that he rarely alludes to any of the figures in the sublime tradition. Why devote so much space to a discussion of Longinus's treatise, it might be asked, if Mallarmé seems never to have read it? The answer is as basic as our choice of critical methodology. We do not propose to examine theories of the sublime with a view to eliciting some chain of historical influence—that of Longinus on the eighteenth-century theorists, say; of Kant on the Romantics, or of anyone on Mallarmé. Such an undertaking is beyond our competence. Moreover, the results of a study of historical influence seem likely in the present case to be trifling, since the sublime is not a phenomenon which lends itself to scientific observation. There is no body of factual knowledge about the sublime to which succeeding generations of critics might have added their own findings. Consequently it is impossible to ascertain how much the treatment of a given aspect of sublimity by one author—of height, for example, or power or terror—owes to its treatment by another. Impossible, that is, unless a distinction between linear and what might be called ambient influence is made. By the latter we understand the climate of intellectual and aesthetic opinion in which individual sensibilities have their being. This looser notion of influence will entitle us to discuss Mallarmé's poetics in connection with, for instance, Kant's "Analytic of the Sublime," on the grounds that, whether or not Mallarmé ever actually sat down and pored over that tract, his exposure to its contents in some form is beyond reasonable question, German metaphysical philosophy having enjoyed a considerable vogue in French Symbolist circles.[2] Likewise when we come to discuss Coleridge and Wordsworth's views on the sublime, our conclusions, insofar as they may imply an influence exerted by these two on Mallarmé, will be sanctioned by the general observations, that Romantic theory crossed national boundaries with ease, that English Romantic literature in particular was well received in France after the dazzling trajectory of Byron over Europe, that certain points of Romantic aesthetic doctrine—notably those arising from speculation about the nature of the sublime—were given their fullest expression in the writings of Coleridge, Wordsworth, Hazlitt and De Quincey, and that Mallarmé, both as teacher and journalist, took a professional interest in English studies—an inconclusive but by no means negligible point. From this kind of circumstantial evidence, obviously, only vague and much-qualified inferences can legitimately be drawn; but it is important that we retain the right to draw them, since our analysis, though for the most part resting on another principle of criticism, will yet depend in some degree on the assumption that the sublime was not exempt from diachronic change. The need for an historical perspective will become especially clear when the sublime is considered in its relation to two questions on which the prevailing intelligent opinion of Mallarmé's day differed markedly from that of his predecessors'. These are the question of the suitable or tolerable proportion of irony to enthusiasm in art and aesthetic experience; and the question of the intellectual respectability of religious faith (or, more basically, of the status of God).

Our procedure in the first part of this study, however, has been to compare a number of theories of the sublime synchronically, rather than as stages in an historical progress. This task was complicated by the lack of a consistent terminology of the sublime. Since the object of signification is nothing less elusive than a superlative state of mind or of the spirit, it is not surprising that it should have been more often evoked with metaphors from the natural world than considered as a thing in itself. One result of this has been a tradition of disagreement about whether the rhetorical and natural sublimes can be independently viewed. The scholarly controversy surrounding the publication of Samuel Monk's *The Sublime* in 1935 brought this tradition to a head; our account of it will be found in chapter nine. A more conspicuous result of the sublime's intangibility, however, is the need which most of its commentators seem to have felt, to emphasize the difficulty of their task, and then to substitute for a rational criterion a private intuition of sublimity. This substitution has been made with more or less frankness and display of moral delicacy. It is a measure of Matthew Arnold's fairness in argument, for example, that, notwithstanding his wish to discourage the tendency to prize brilliant passages at the expense of formal values, he was led in his later criticism to acknowledge the appeal of the sublime, and even to exempt it from the requirement of submitting to definition: " 'the grand style'—Longinus' sublimity, as interpreted with the help of Joshua Reynolds' *Discourses*— . . . 'is the last matter in the world for verbal definition to deal with adequately'; 'one must feel it in order to know what it is.' "[4] Benedetto Croce, with bold paradox, transformed this weakness into a principle of his aesthetics: "So we must leave writers and speakers free to define the sublime . . . on every occasion as they please and as may suit the end they have in view. And if an empirical definition of universal validity be demanded, we can but submit this one: The sublime . . . is *everything* that is or shall be so *called* by those who have employed or shall employ [this] *word.*"[5] A contemporary writer sums up the difficulty by observing, that " 'Sublime' has a long history of imprecise meanings (though everyone always seemed to know what was meant)."[6]

It might, on the contrary, be maintained that much of the disagreement about the proper application of the word "sublime" in the eighteenth and nineteenth centuries sprang from a sense that its earlier application had been too narrow, its meaning too precise. Longinus's *hupsous*, and his treatise as a whole, were taken to refer solely to an effect of rhetoric. The gradual extension of the term to denote an order of natural phenomena, and a psychological state not necessarily produced by literary means, can be seen as the slow defeat of an accepted usage. This view helps to explain the fact that the word "sublime" is often missing from those contexts where its appearance might most be expected. Several critics have noticed its absence from Addison's essay on "Pleasures of the Imagination," which contains one of the first descriptions of the natural sublime.[7] John Dennis, the inventor of an early psychological theory of sublimity, "described his Alpine experiences in a now famous letter without once resorting to the word *sublime*."[8] Thomas De Quincey did little more than give eloquent expression to a commonplace when he said that "in Milton only, first and last, is the power of the sublime revealed. In Milton only does this great agency blaze and glow as a furnace kept up to a white heat—without suspicion of collapse."[9] Yet Samuel Monk considered it "a strange paradox that the most sublime of English poets should not have caught from Longinus the suggestion of the sublime as the expression of ultimate values in art, beyond the reach of rhetoric. . . . He did not; and it was left to the propounders of an adolescent aesthetic in the next century to find in John Milton's poems . . . the supreme illustration of whatever particular type of the sublime they advocated."[10]

We shall dispute the reading of Longinus that led Monk to speak of a "strange paradox" here. Before doing so, however, we should take what advantage is offered by the example of Reynolds, Arnold, Croce and every other critic whose final criterion of sublimity lay beyond his ability to articulate, by claiming the benefit of the doubt for those passages which we ourselves shall adduce as specimens of the sublime. In every such case an attempt will be made to demonstrate that the passage conforms to some aspect of the syncretic theory of sublimity to be outlined in this part—for it is our contention that the sublime is *not* an indefinable quality, but one that arises inevitably when certain conditions are met. Nevertheless, it should be borne in mind that one person's transport can excite another's scorn, and that the step of appealing to the reader's sympathy may prove difficult to avoid. Coleridge was among the first to recognize what C. D. Thorpe calls "the power of mind to find sublimity in objects not sublime to others."[11] In a letter of the year 1800 he wrote:

> At times I dwell on man with such reverence, resolve all his follies and superstitions into such grand primary laws of intellect, and in such wise so contemplate them as ever-varying incarnations of the Eternal Life—that the Llama's dung-pellet, or the cowtail which the dying Brahmin clutches convulsively become sanctified and sublime by the feelings which cluster round them.[12]

The lesson was more harshly repeated when the passage in Coleridge's "Hymn before Sunrise" that "best describe[s] sublimity as [he] conceived it" was condemned by his close ally Wordsworth "as a specimen of the Mock Sublime."[13] The former's conviction "that it was the image and utterance of Thoughts and Emotions in which there was no Mockery" could not ensure that the passage would be read in a spirit of sympathetic enthusiasm, or charitable indulgence, or that someone who had not experienced the grandiose thoughts and emotions that attended the creation of the poem, would incline rather to approve its ambitious intention, than to censure its extravagance. The occasion for this disagreement was a passage in which sublime feelings are directly attributed to a vision of God. As our discussion of the religious sublime will show, the clash of irony and enthusiasm is most violent when the latter impulse has a specifically devotional cast.

Chapter Two

Longinus a Romantic? Importance of social considerations in his work.

Since the mid-eighteenth century, when Longinus's treatise *Peri Hupsous* (περι ὕψους) became well known, critics have tended to adopt one of two distinct views of the nature of his work. Either it was primarily a manual of practical advice to rhetoricians, dealing with a special aspect of their art, and resembling numerous other classical studies of the high style in everything but its readability and the surprising[1] assortment of illustrations it contains; or it was a text *sui generis*, the only work of antiquity to foreshadow the Romantic belief, that emotional intensity, and irrational appeal, not the harmonious disposition of unagitating parts, were the hallmarks of great literature. The second of these views has predominated since the publication, thirty years ago, of M. H. Abrams's influential study *The Mirror and the Lamp*. Longinus's "reliance on ecstasy instead of analysis as the criterion of excellence," his "tendency . . . to move from the quality of a work to its genesis in the powers and state of mind . . . of its author" make him, according to Abrams, "the exemplar and source of many elements of romantic theory."[2]

Certainly, the famous passages in *Peri Hupsous* in which the sublime is described as "the echo of a great soul" that fills the audience with a sense of "joy and vaunting" bear out this reading, as does Longinus's preference for flawed works of genius over the most finished productions of mediocrity.[3] But it is a reading which dwells on a single thread in the argument of *Peri Hupsous* in order to provide the Romantics with a spiritual forefather, and one which, at the same time, assures the symmetry of Mr. Abrams's literary history. The opinions of Romantic critics on Longinus's work are not mentioned. Abrams remarks that "strangely, the triumph of his perspective only occurred when Longinus himself had lost his earlier prestige and was rarely cited by practicing critics."[4] This circumstance seems less strange if our explanation of the low occurrence of the word "sublime" in the nineteenth century is adopted—an explanation which the following quotations from Wordsworth and Coleridge fully support, even as they cast strong doubt on the view of Longinus as a Romantic *avant la lettre*:

> One is surprised that it should have been supposed for a moment, that Longinus writes upon the sublime, even in our vague and popular sense of the word. What is there in Sappho's ode that has any affinity with the sublimity of Ezekiel or Isaiah, or even of Homer and Aeschylus? Longinus treats of animated, empassioned, energetic, or, if you will, elevated writing. Of these, abundant instances are to be found in Aeschylus and Homer; but nothing would be easier to show, both by positive and negative proof, that his *hupsous* when translated "sublimity" deceives the English reader, by substituting an etymology for a translation. Much of what I observe you call sublime, I should denominate grand or dignified.[5]

> Longinus was no very profound critic; but he was no blunderer. Of the energetic, of the language of high excitement, elevated from passion . . . [Sappho's ode] was, is, and

> probably ever will be, the most perfect specimen. But as to sublime you might as well call it blue or small-poxed.[6]

That the sublime had acquired such complete independence from "the language of high excitement," from energy and from passion in the schemes of these critics, was a consequence, we shall argue, of certain qualitative changes which, since Longinus's day, the Ideal—the unattainable object of sublime aspiration—had sustained. Wordsworth's claim, that "nothing would be easier to show" than the difference between his sublimity and Longinus's *hupsous*, should also be noted for the presumption on which it is based, that even so rare and extreme an effect of art as the sense of the sublime can be transmitted in language as a matter of course; can be encoded and decoded without fear that its essence has been lost in the process;—for the presumption, in short, against which Mallarmé was to rebel, that the ideal is not ineffable.

The quotations invite us to reexamine the rival interpretation of Longinus's work. This has been upheld in recent years by Malcolm Ware, who asserts that Longinus "considered sublimity for the most part a rhetorical and stylistic device [not dependent] upon intense emotions"[7]; by D. A. Russell in the introduction to his translation of the work,[8] and by Jules Brody, who asserts that Longinus "wrote a practical treatise."[9] Brody warns the reader of his learned study *Boileau and Longinus* that "in using these words ['sublimity' and 'the Sublime'] I shall be careful to ignore the altogether extraneous suggestions . . . lent them by Burke and heightened by the Romantics, and shall insist exclusively on their reference to what Longinus called 'a certain elevated and outstanding quality in literary style.' "[10]

A good case for this interpretation of Longinus can be made from the text of *Peri Hupsous.* In chapter one the author indeed distinguishes between the workaday rhetoric whose purpose is to "persuade the hearers," and the "elevated language" that does not so much "persuade" as "entrance" them.[11] But the modern acceptation of rhetoric as the "art of persuasion" should not lead us rashly to conclude, that Longinus's "elevated language" must be something entirely different. On the contrary, the rest of chapter one suggests that the end of sublimity is to "reveal the full power of the speaker" in order that he may "win for [himself] an eternity of fame."[12] The reader may already suspect that Longinus's *hupsous* is rooted in considerations which it is no less proper to characterize as political than as aesthetic.

This suspicion is confirmed in the following chapters, which are devoted to a minute discussion of the use of rhetorical figures. The compatibility of sublimity and rhetoric in Longinus is wholly unlike the relation that was to obtain between these categories in the aesthetic systems of the Romantics. The nineteenth-century depreciation of eloquence as a sort of spurious poetry, and the view that rhetorical contrivance invariably betrays a lack of inspiration, is attested in the remarks of such dissimilar writers as Mill, Shelley, Poe and Verlaine.[13] The list could be indefinitely prolonged.

It is not necessary to maintain that, because all of these writers undoubtedly possessed rhetorical skills in a high degree, and exerted those skills with greatest success precisely where their work appears most natural and spontaneous, they must therefore have been misrepresenting the creative process, or deluding themselves. What is important is the immeasurable loftiness of the poetic ideal their remarks imply, its essential independence from the executive aspects of literature. The mutual incomprehension and divorce of poet and society which results from the unearthly role of the former in this ideology, is well known.

In Longinus matters are quite otherwise. The test of a sublime passage is whether it gives "an intelligent and well-read man . . . food for reflection."[14] Nor is this man exceptional, since "sublimity in all its truth and beauty exists in such works as please all men at all times."[15] The sublime orator no less than the most phlegmatic member of his audience participated in a community where the sentence of exile constituted the heaviest penalty of law. Since sublimity was defined by the intensity of public enthusiasm it excited, rather than by its fidelity to some private ideal of the poet's, the latter was guilty of no misconduct in striving to enhance the effect of his conceptions by disclosing them with an adroit use of rhetorical figures. So, throughout this text, Longinus advises his young pupil, not to *be* natural, but to *appear* to be so. The instructions are, not to avoid the use of "cunning artifice," but to take care that it remains "out of sight." "For a display of feeling is more effective when it *seems* not to be premeditated on the part of the speaker, but to have arisen from the occasion; and this method of asking questions and providing your own answers *gives the appearance* of being a natural outburst of feeling."[16]

Public approval, then, is the indispensable adjunct of sublimity in Longinus. The effects of this circumstance are far-reaching. In the first place, the audience has an active role in determining the character of the literary product. The modern notion of the "monumentality"[17] of the text, so well suited to a social organization in which the reader privately enjoys what the author wrote in solitude, requires some modification to accommodate the reading of Demosthenes's *De Corona* in which Longinus stresses, that "we must take into account the place, the manner, the circumstances, and the motive"[18]—all matters which, properly speaking, lie outside the text. But the audience also makes its presence felt at an earlier stage in the production of the text, by constraining the author to keep the probable reception of his work in mind even while he is creating it. He must not lose sight of the possibility that, in giving license to his imagination, he may render himself ridiculous. He must submit his ideas to the scrutiny of a censorious inner eye, which tests them for their susceptibility to public derision. Hence the injunction to "remain sober . . . even in orgies of the imagination," and the opinion, several times expressed, that sublime passages can be "repeatedly examined" in "the light of day."[19] The metaphor of daylight admirably conveys Longinus's matter-of-fact attitude towards the sublime—an attitude and a metaphor completely unlike the reverence and obnubilation of the Romantics. The advantage of this public criterion of sublimity is, that when the audience grants its approval, it does so wholeheartedly, and the division between it and the speaker is removed: "we are filled with a proud exaltation and a sense of vaunting joy, just as though we had ourselves produced what we had heard."[20] The arrangement is favorable to the creation of intimate multitudes; but it seems to entail a certain chastening of the artist's ideal,[21] at least by the standards of subsequent ages when the right to express refractory views has been more fiercely asserted, and the approval of society more arrogantly spurned.

Chapter Three

The measure of Longinus's idealism. His practical approach to the sublime—a moderate experience. His conception of language "unliterary" by Mallarmé's definition. His conception of the ideal not modern.

Before examining that ideal more closely, however, we should correct the one-sidedness of the view of Longinus just proposed, by observing, that despite the quantity of advice he offers about the proper use of rhetorical figures, and his evident desire to preserve the speaker's dignity at the very pitch of his enthusiasm, he nonetheless lays great emphasis on the matter of sublime discourse. So the "first and most important" qualification of the orator is his "ability to form grand conceptions": "nobility of soul plays the most important part of . . . all."[1] It is undoubtedly this emphasis that accounts for the revival of *Peri Hupsous* in the eighteenth century, and that has led so many critics to adopt the view that, in Longinus, the sublime is "more a matter of content . . . than of form. Any subject which can genuinely excite is capable of being handled in a 'sublime' way."[2] We should also point out, that in his chapter on "Imagery and the Power of the Imagination" the author distinguishes between poetry, which "display[s] a good deal of romantic exaggeration and everywhere exceed[s] the bounds of credibility," and oratory, for which a scrupulous "adherence to reality and truth" is required.[3] Sublime effects are not necessarily devoted to civil ends, nor do they only occur in the course of a public harangue. But our basic point, that Longinus's conception of language as a public commodity explains the relatively moderate character of his *hupsous*, holds good.

Longinus resembles the great majority of writers on the sublime in this, that he prefers to illustrate his conception of the subject with quotations, and with lively metaphors of his own invention, than to undertake the more arduous task of deducing the psychological operations which result in the sense of the sublime. Perhaps the intellectual tools necessary for such an undertaking did not then exist; certainly, among writers of a much more sophisticated and technically accomplished age, only Kant and Coleridge produced convincing theories of the latter description. But the Greek author's practice of suggesting, rather than spelling out his points is no matter for regret to us, since it will facilitate the comparison to be made in part two of the present study, between the themes and imagery of Mallarmé's writings, and those which have persistently recurred in the literature of the sublime tradition.

Longinus's chapter on "Plato and Lysias" and its immediate sequel, the chapter on "Sublimity and Literary Fame," together comprise the most striking, because the most concentrated, instance of his ability to reconcile an aesthetic ideal which he characterizes as "divine," with a fundamentally material conception of the purposes and capabilities of language. He begins with a celebration of "those godlike authors" who, inspired by "an unconquerable passion for all that is great and for all that is more divine than ouselves," "showed no respect for detailed accuracy."[4] Their sublime works are then compared to the grand phenomena of nature in a passage which Boileau presumably had in mind when he claimed, that "en parlant du sublime, [Longin] est lui-même très sublime,"[5] or Alexander Pope when he affirmed, that Longinus is "himself that great Sublime he draws":[6]

> This is why, by some sort of natural instinct, we admire, not, surely, the small streams, beautifully clear though they may be, and useful too, but the Nile, the Danube, the Rhine, and even more than these the Ocean. The little fire that we have kindled ourselves, clear and steady as its flame may be, does not strike us with as much awe as the heavenly fires, in spite of their often being shrouded in darkness; nor do we think it a greater marvel than the craters of Etna, whose eruptions throw up from their depths rocks and even whole mountains, and at times pour out rivers of that pure Titanian fire. In all such circumstances, I would say only this, that men hold cheap that is useful and necessary, and always reserve their admiration for what is out of the ordinary.[7]

Then comes the surprising first line of chapter 36: "Now with regard to authors of genius, *whose grandeur always has some bearing on questions of utility and profit*" (italics added).

This remark, thrown out carelessly in an aside as if its truth were beyond dispute, appears at first to contradict the lofty conception of sublimity outlined in the preceding chapter; in fact it supports it. For the repeated allusions to "those godlike authors," "these demigods" who "rise above the human level" and approach "the majestic mind of God"[8] must not blind the modern reader, with his presumptions concerning the great divorce of Christian theology, to the comfortable integration of heaven and earth in Longinus's system. There is awe, and elation, but there is no trouble in his sublimity, no sense that it is too much to bear. In the passage cited above, the heavenly fires are awesome "*in spite* of their often being shrouded in darkness" (italics added), not, as later theorists would argue, *because* they are so shrouded. In contradistinction to the ideas of terror and danger in the sublime moment as described by Burke—ideas which increase the subject's sense of his relative smallness and vulnerability, and therefore also his sense that the disproportion between himself and the source of his terror is very great—Longinus gives us the picture of a happy relationship between man and the "great festival" of life to which he has been summoned. Far from threatening to annihilate him, the sublime encourages man to believe that he is a "creature of no mean or ignoble quality."[9] True, Longinus says that "the entire universe does not satisfy the contemplation and thought that lie within the scope of human endeavour; our ideas often go beyond the boundaries by which we are circumscribed."[10] But there is no suggestion that these outlands of "contemplation and thought" are different *in kind* from the real world of oceans and volcanoes. The human spirit in its uttermost extension does not shake off a concern for "utility and profit": that concern like an anchor saves the artist in his "highest flight" from the folly of an Icarian ascent.

From this domestication of the sublime results a sense of safety completely unlike the fearful Burkean and Romantic attitudes. A spirit of public emulation is encouraged, and the glory redounding to the authors of sublime works is emphasized at least as much as the sublimity of the works themselves. Hence the repeated admonitions against tumidity, false sentiment, frigidity and other errors of tact: the author who commits them imperils his chances of securing "an eternity of fame." "And indeed the fight for fame and the crown of victory are noble and very well worth the winning." Longinus accordingly advises the aspiring author to ask himself the question, "What kind of hearing should I get from all future ages if I wrote this?" In so doing he will bring his writings nearer to "such perfection as [will] ensure their fame in later ages."[11]

Other aspects of Longinus's sublime reflect his endorsement of a social criterion of aesthetic success, his reluctance to stray too far from the fold. The gifts of genius are at one point likened to "great wealth," at another to "riches"; and "copiousness" is among the chief attributes of the sublime orator.[12] The following passage, in which he seems to deny the suitability of wealth as a metaphor for sublime language, is ambiguous.

> Thus riches, honours, reputation, sovereignty, and all the other trappings of a showy splendour, would not seem to a sensible man to be great blessings, since contempt for them is itself regarded as a considerable virtue; and indeed people admire those who possess them less than those who could have them but are high-minded enough to despise them.[13]

What is important here is not the high-minded rejection of wealth and prestige but the reasons given for that rejection. Longinus does not say that contempt for riches is a virtue. He says that it "is regarded" as such. The incentive to despise "honours, reputation," etc., is the knowledge that "people admire" those who despise them, or rather, "those who could have them" but reject them. The passage suggests a situation in which the highly regarded and admired repudiators of admiration and regard are well-known for that repudiation, which is generally agreed to be admirable.

A contrast to Mallarmé may be drawn here. Longinus's "elevated language," though continually shrugging off the finery of rhetoric, and never stooping to what Conrad called "the miserable vanity of a catching phrase,"[14] still conforms to Mallarmé's definition of unliterary language, by remaining always subservient to "questions of utility and profit," and displaying the characteristics of a particularly precious intellectual currency:

> Narrer, enseigner, même décrire, cela va et encore qu'à chacun suffirait peut-être pour échanger la pensée humaine, de prendre ou de mettre dans la main d'autrui une pièce de monnaie, l'emploi élémentaire du discours dessert l'universel *reportage* dont, la littérature exceptée, participe tout entre les genres d'écrits contemporains.[15]

Elsewhere Longinus uses other metaphors to convey his

idea of the sublime in literature. In two separate passages he compares great writing to statuary, although in the second case his conclusion seems to militate against our argument. In chapter thirty he says that "words finely used are in truth the very light of thought."[16] The metaphor of light, however, is firmly integrated in a context of heavy substantives ("grandeur, beauty, mellowness, weight, force, power") which contradict its *sème* of immateriality, and which cause it to function, not as the vivid crystallization of the passage's drift, but as a slightly inapposite ornament. The light is not evoked for its own qualities, but in order to play over "the finest statues" that precede it, and to become their "*living* voice" (italics added). Sublimity here is the apanage of human beings and their effigies, not the terrible radiance from an ideal world. It is a public matter of swaying the Greek burghers with "grand diction" and "high-sounding words."[17] In chapter thirty-six, however, the author maintains that "in statues we look for the likeness of a man, whereas in literature . . . we look for something transcending the human." The metaphor that so well conveyed the virtues of an "Parnassian" style (as G. M. Hopkins later called it)[18]—the gravity and dignity, the imperturabable measure and conclusive form—is inadequate as a means of suggesting the dynamic properties of language, for which purpose Mallarmé and others would subsequently adopt the neighboring metaphor of the dance.[19] So much we are prepared to admit. But how far does Longinus's search for something transcending the human take him? He rejects "the likeness of a man" in favor of various "heaven-sent gifts" which Demosthenes and other "demigods" possess: "lifelike passions, copiousness, readiness, speed . . . and vehemence."[20] These gifts will certainly enable the orator to "put down all his rivals";[21] but they seem remarkably ill-suited for any other purpose. They would constitute a positive hindrance to someone intent on approaching an abstract ideal: one fears that, at the last moment, as the doors of the tabernacle begin to open, Demosthenes will burst out with a speech of impassioned eloquence, denouncing the machinations of his political enemies.

The matter may be put more succinctly. In Longinus's system, as in the systems of later theorists, the artist tries to render the quality of an ideal which, despite his best efforts, remains more or less aloof.[22] Setting aside all variations in emphasis and definition, and taking the term in its loosest sense only, the "sublime" stands for an extreme degree of success in this attempt. Its precise character, however, and the extent to which a particular emotion such as terror or joy predominates in association with it, depends on how unlike, how far apart, how incompatible the real and ideal are allowed to be. One of the contentions of this study is that Mallarmé's poetic theory and practice reflect an evaluation of the dissimilarity of these extremes *ne plus ultra.* But in Longinus, the real and ideal commingle freely. On the one hand, the artist can aspire with some optimism to the status of a demigod. He can embody the ideal in his own person, and array his reputation in the "intricate folds and sweeping draperies" of his art (as Hazlitt said of Sir Thomas Browne).[23] Since this transfiguration is not impossible for an "artist of genius"; since the ideal can be attained "by a sort of natural instinct,"[24] and with relative ease, the sublime carries little suggestion of terror, and none at all of despair, in Longinus. "For some emotions can be found that are mean and not in the least sublime, such as pity, grief and *fear.*"[25] Elsewhere his imagery of thunderbolts and whirlwinds implies that the audience should feel a measure of salutary fear as it is being "swept off its feet"—but never so much as to menace the conviction that, even under such circumstances, we remain "creatures of no mean or ignoble quality." On the contrary, the ideal is near and alluring, and "implants in our souls an unconquerable passion"[26] for itself. The artist's enthusiasm is qualified only by his apprehension of ridicule; he does not know the "irony . . . born when division intrudes on poetic hope."[27]

Small surprise, then, that the ideal should be so often

personified in Longinus's treatise, as it is in the lines about Poseidon which allegedly "represent the divine nature . . . pure, majestic and undefiled."[28] The presence here of several organic, not to say grotesque details, such as: "the monsters of the deep came from their hiding places and gambolled about him, for they knew their lord," goes some way towards explaining the contempt in which Coleridge held "the Religion of Greece and Rome": "the quarrels of Jupiter and Juno, the whimpering of wounded Venus, and the jokes of the celestials on the lameness of Vulcan"[24] represented for him a moral system and a conception of divinity not much above the level of sordid anecdote. The contrast between the ideal to be inferred from Longinus's account of poets and orators plying the trade of sublime authorship, so to speak, and that which Christianity has given to even the most heretical artists of modern times—an ideal at once more personal and more abstract—was first drawn by Coleridge:

> The more I think, the more I am convinced that the greatest of differences is produced when in the one case the feelings are worked upon thro' the Imagination and the Imagination thro' definite Forms (i.e. the Religion of Greece and Rome); and in the other cases where the Feelings are worked upon by Hopes and Fears purely individual, and the Imagination is kept barren in definite Forms and only in cooperation with the Understanding labours after an obscure and indefinite Vastness—this is Christianity.[30]

De Quincey made a similar point when he said that "the Grecians had apparently no word"[31] for the kind of sublimity exemplified in Milton and in the prophetic books of the Old Testament. Longinus, too, seems to have been impressed by the idea of limitless power transforming itself into real form which the sentences of fiat in Genesis convey—"Let there be light," etc.—; and the fact that a writer of the first century B.C. should have chosen to illustrate his conception of the sublime by this passage is sufficiently remarkable for one editor to suggest on the strength of it, that the author of *Peri Hupsous* was probably not a Greek at all, but an Alexandrian Jew.[32] Nothing in Longinus's brief remarks on the passage, however, indicates that he imagined the "Divine Being" of the Hebrews to be anything less of a concrete patriarch, anything more nearly approaching to an abstract principle or disembodied ideal, than the figures of his own mythology.

Coleridge's proposed distinction is especially interesting on another score. It is easy to grant that the parterres of Olympus are not so far above our heads as John Martin's *Plains of Heaven*, say, or that a divine order the figures of which are subject to every human failing, and guilty of the most flagitious crimes—of rape, murder, incest and patricide, as well as drunkenness and sloth—that such a divine order offers by its example little incitement to the strenuous sort of spiritual comportment whose expression in artistic form we are accustomed to describe as sublime. But the question remains whether even the most austere imagination can altogether dispense with "definite Forms." In the passage quoted above Coleridge alludes to "an obscure and indefinite Vastness" which the imagination glimpses only "in cooperation with the Understanding." (The latter faculty corresponds very closely to Kant's *Zusammenfassung*, as we shall see.) By its frequent use in the landscape poetry of the late eighteenth century, however, and because it had been the subject of a well-known controversy in France,[33] the adjective "vast" (from which Coleridge's abstract noun derives) was firmly linked, by the time he received it, to certain topographical notions which, far from repudiating, he willingly adopted. On the occasions in his poems and letters when he successfully encodes the structure of the sublime, he does so by applying such words as "obscure" and "indefinite" to nouns representing things. His apprehension of "boundless or endless allness," his "idea of infinity" must be tapped by the image of a "cloudcapped mountain," or "a huge Valley with rocks," or "a Sea of huge motionless Waves," or a Miltonian host of angels,[34] in order to acquire for the reader an interest more compelling than that of biographical detail. When, on the contrary, he deliberately erases the elements of a recognizable décor from his poem, and invites us to contemplate "the Invisible alone," we find it easy to refuse (as did Wordsworth). The problem is not that the invisible and the infinite are unfit subjects for poetry, but that some means of suggesting them more sophisticated than Coleridge's has to be found—some technique less dependent on the presumed transparency of language, and which will forbid the expedient of placing a blockish abstract noun in the middle of one's verse. "Suggérer, voilà le rêve."[35] In the syntactical sleights and obliquites of Mallarmé's poetry, a solution of this superior kind is revealed. No one has better illustrated the truth of Thomas Weiskel's observation, that "in the case of poetic imagery . . . it is notoriously difficult to draw a clear line between the image as perception and as sign standing for the nonsensible or the unimaginable—a fact that accounts for a history of quarrels over what is or is not sublime."[36]

There is a danger that the nontechnical language in which we have just distinguished between the sublime passages in Coleridge and those which are not sublime, may have created the impression that that distinction involved a personal value judgment of our own. This is not the case. The coincidence of Coleridge's successful attempts at the sublime with his employment of the vocabulary of natural description, and the coincidence of his failures with the occasions on which he relied on the evocative power of abstract nouns, can be explained in the more objective language of the theory of the sublime developed hereinafter as a function of the balance or imbalance of the motives of irony and enthusiasm, that characterize the subject's relation to the ideal. Our definition of those terms, however, must await the completion of a preliminary comparison of texts by several authors that illustrate different attitudes to the ideal, and different outcomes of the attempt at sublimity. Rather than introduce the main components of our theory prematurely, we have expressed the above distinction in terms less proof against the charge of subjective preference than those which we shall employ in our discussion of Mallarmé.

We shall continue to refer to Longinus's treatise in later sections of this study, where his position on matters of thematic emphasis will stand out in contrast to the positions of other writers. For the present it is enough to note, that the author of *Peri Hupsous* as we have described him bears little resemblance to the stock figure reproduced by so many literary historians. The picture of a frenzied bacchant of criticism, transported by the rush of his ideas, is a false likeness, whose subject's own fairly conventional features (his public standard of aesthetic success and belief that art should serve the common weal; his concern for the artist's public dignity, to be maintained by a constant observance of the amenities; his conception of an ideal belonging to an ontology that includes no atemporal dimension, and which therefore never expresses itself as an abstraction, but always in natural or anthropomorphic imagery) have been glossed over by a set of equally conventional but demonstrably less pertinent strokes, intended to point up his superficial resemblance to the Romantics. But leaving this, we come to consider an antagonist of the eighteenth-century religious sublime, in the shape of Samuel Johnson.

Chapter Four

The sublime of Dr. Johnson. Words cannot do justice to the ideal: the necessity of silence.

Although his remarks on "the grand or lofty stile"[1] are less haphazard than Longinus's, being connected to the whole body of his aesthetic judgments in a rigorously logical fashion, and with a grasp of organizational principles which the Greek author did not command, Johnson's idea of the sublime is chiefly interesting for its limitations. These arise from his distaste for the literary expressions of religious faith, and his belief that the rational faculties should not be too often supplanted by strong emotion. The question of how far the artist's prerogative should extend into the realm of the ideal—of how much he should say, and how much leave unsaid—a question the answer to which depends on whether one accepts the proposition that the ideal is God—a God in whom one believes, not for the purpose of creating literature, but in order to save one's soul; a God whose wrath is too terrible to write poems about, and whose promise of salvation is extended only in exchange for one's silence on His account, one's reverent submission to His will—this question is central to Mallarmé's thought, and will be explored in a digression of some length. But first, let us identify the innovative points of Johnson's argument concerning the rhetorical sublime.

Five definitions of the adjective "sublime" are given in Johnson's *Dictionary*, of which only one refers to a quality of style. As J. H. Hagstrum says, he "often used the word literally and metaphorically for anything that was lofty."[2] The sole definition of the substantive, however, amounts to "little more than the traditional rhetorical meaning."[3] Where, then, is the novelty of Johnson's usage? Certainly not in his insistence on the compatibility of "easy poetry" and the sublime, although that insistence is characteristic of the man who, in Hazlitt's words, "required that the string should rather be relaxed than tightened," and who "refused to be roused to any keen agony of thought."[4] Ease of diction was already implicit in Longinus's metaphors of gushing eloquence and unconstrained power. It reappeared in the "naïveté de langage" recommended by Boileau, and in the "simplicité de style" which that critic considered essential to sublime discourse.[5] Nor does Johnson much surprise us when he proclaims the "grandeur of generality": "Sublimity is produced by aggregation, and littleness by dispersion. Great thoughts are always general, and consist . . . in descriptions not descending to minuteness."[6] Longinus had already shown that "entire accuracy runs the risk of descending to triviality, whereas in the grand manner, as in the possession of great wealth, something is bound to be neglected."[7] In the eighteenth century this taste for a *beau désordre* in letters was justified on the grounds that it reflected Nature's own prodigality and dishevelment. Frederick Stover has argued[8] that the tendency to generalize in descriptions of sublime natural scenes was a sign that, from an aesthetic point of view, the precise delineation of such scenes had ceased to matter so much as the quality and force of their impact on the spectator. (In part two we shall consider how Mallarmé improved on this technique in his attempt to "peindre, non la chose, mais l'effet qu'elle produit.")[9] So widely upheld as a means of creating sublime effects had generalization become, that it was not before some twenty-five years had elapsed, and the standards of taste had been radically changed, that William Blake could declare: "All Sublimity is founded on Minute Discrimination . . . Particular Detail is the Foundation of the Sublime."[10] Yet even in 1806 Blake's position was eccentric. His contemporaries no less than their fathers were inclined to generalize in the grand manner, and evinced considerable relish for "descriptions not descending to minuteness." When details are too numerous or too intrinsically interesting, Johnson and others seem to have felt, the attention is dissipated, and "Great Thoughts" cannot be entertained.

The literary effects available through the accumulation of detail are, however, too valuable to be thrown away in a movement of fastidious recoil from the danger that, in attempting to secure them, one may lapse into triviality. That movement, and the impulse which inspires it, belong to Longinus's category of "negative virtues."[11] For if the test of a sublime work is its power to overwhelm the reader, why should this not be accomplished by multiplying the number of details, dividing and scattering the reader's wits among them, and terrifying him with the idea that a state of chaos is about to supervene? This is the situation which Longinus described in his chapter on "Inversion." By interposing a great number of subordinate clauses between the principal clauses of his sentence, the orator "induces in his hearer the fear that the whole structure of the sentence will fall to pieces, and compels him in his agitation to share in the risk the speaker is taking."[12] This technique was one of Mallarmé's favorite resources in his pursuit of the sublime. It is evident not only in "Un Coup de dés," where his abandonment of linear discourse in favor of an "éparpillement en frissons articulés"[13] of language is expected (as he said) to command the reader's "puissance d'enthousiasme."[14] It is also evident in his prose writings, where the subordination of clauses and parts of speech is sometimes not plainly indicated. His tendency to "escamoter les relatifs quand il peut"[15] throws the reader off his guard; and by omitting those elements of logical connection that would enable the reader to grasp his meaning too securely, he achieves the effect which we shall recognize, in chapter nine, as constituting the first stage of the sublime experience.

There is no reason, then, why the "excess on the plane of signifiers"[16] which Kant's mathematical sublime involves, should not rather take the form of details too numerous and too discrete, than of a unity too inclusive, to be grasped. The place assigned to "poetical terrour" in Johnson's description of the sublime is small, however, and the potentially terrifying effects of minute discrimination went entirely unnoticed by him. Those effects, which are obtained by a rhetorical tactic of subverting the reader's equilibrium,[17] would in any case not have appealed to Johnson, who more than any writer was addicted to a style of elaborately balanced thesis and antithesis.

Johnson contributed to the definition of a rhetorical sublime in two ways. First, he modified the concept of a "perfect" sublime, derived originally from Longinus but immediately from Addison, so as to emphasize its formal constitution instead of its source in the mind of the author. For Addison's "nobleness of thoughts" and "magnificence of the words," he substituted the terms "argumentative" and "descriptive" sublimity,[18] and in so doing, removed from the reader's light, so to speak, the obstructive shadow of whichever demigod wrote the passage in question. His second contribution was to stress the "rational admiration" that succeeds "sudden astonishment" in the course of the sublime moment.[19] Johnson's account of this succession is less satisfactory than Kant's, however, because he fails to explain why it should take place. This is perhaps due to the moderate character of his "sudden astonishment" which, although it "fills the whole mind," does not appear to strain it. In Kant, the substitution of "reason's idea of infinity"[20] for the imagination's attempt to picture the unimaginable, is brought about as a last resort, to save the mind from collapse. Johnson's astonishment on the other hand, is not usually a desperate condition, and except in the special cases discussed below, gives way to rational admiration in a calm and stately manner, describing a revolution like that accomplished in any of his periods.

Only in his remarks on Milton and sacred history does Johnson betray a less complacent confidence in his powers of critical analysis, and employ the word "sublime" to denote a literary quality far surpassing that of elevation in its power to exercise and alarm. From the "awful scenes" of heavenly combat in *Paradise Lost* "we recede with reverence" or "shrink with horror."[21] Milton alone among poetical fabulists could thus cow the doctor into suspending his disbelief. Other attempts to "poetize the Scriptures" he termed "profane." For it is the peculiar distinction of sacred history that it

> has been always read with submissive reverence, and an imagination overawed and controlled. We have been accumstomed to acquiesce in the nakedness and simplicity of the authentick narrative, and to repose on its veracity with such humble confidence as suppresses curiosity. . . . All amplification is frivolous and vain.[22]

Johnson is not led to this extreme position by his faith alone. His rejection of devotional poetry, and his belief that the habit of indulging in sublime thoughts may become "a dangerous prevalence of the imagination,"[23] are founded on logic as well. He reasons that since wonder—the mental condition induced by sublime spectacles—"is an effect of ignorance," and since God, the omniscient, is incapable of wondering, man will be "likest God when he is fully aware that too strong a taste for the sublime is a confession of human weakness and ignorance,"[24] and refrains from indulging it.

> Pleasure and terrour are, indeed, the genuine sources of poetry; but poetical pleasure must be such as human imagination can, at least, conceive; and poetical terrour, such

> as human strength and fortitude may combat. The good and evil of eternity are too ponderous for the wings of wit; the mind sinks under them in passive helplessness, content with calm belief and humble adoration.[25]

The conception of the ideal which prompts Johnson to this act of renunciation is different from Mallarmé's in an important respect. Johnson's faith (a form of enthusiasm peculiarly resistant to the mitigating influence of irony) leads him to regard the ideal as more real than any thing. It is the object of enthusiastic devotion whose reality is not diminished by its immateriality. The reality of the ideal is to be proved in Johnson's personal salvation. Hence his attitude to the ideal is characterized by an enthusiasm too complete for him to allow it to dissipate in the practice of literature—a practice which (with respect to the ideal) is characterized by the art of compromise. In Mallarmé's attitude to the ideal, on the other hand, the principle of irony predominates. His emphasis is characteristically on the nothingness of the ideal ("le Rien qui est la vérité,")[26] and on the disappointment which invariably attends the directing of personal enthusiasm towards it. Attracted, however, to an ideal of whose unreality he is convinced, he is at liberty to breach the perfection of his silence and employ his enthusiasm in a literary celebration of the ideal—or more exactly, a celebration of the irony of his perception of the ideal. Against the barrenness (in terms of a literary treatment of the ideal) of Johnson's enthusiasm, then, may be set the fertility of Mallarmé's irony.

The matter is more complicated than that, however. Mallarmé's priestly attitudes, and his complaints of sterility, are indications that the motives of irony and enthusiasm were not so happily adjusted in him as we have suggested. But we have yet to fashion the descriptive tools necessary for the examination of his prose writings to be conducted in part two. The next step in that process is to obtain a clearer understanding of the effects of a literary indulgence of enthusiasm, as represented by the practitioners of the religious sublime.

Chapter Five

Contrast of Johnson to the practitioners of the "religious" sublime. The ideal takes a material form, of which they may speak. Uneasiness of their position.

No episode in the history of speculation on the nature of the sublime has been more amply documented—no body of superseded thought more eagerly and contentiously raked over—no conflict of critical doctrines more belligerently resumed by scholars more stubbornly indifferent to the obsolescence of the causes they espouse, than that which began around 1700 with the publication of works by Addison and Dennis,[1] and culiminated some sixty years later in the atmosphere of furor, amazement and indignation, which the appearance of Edmund Burke's *Inquiry* produced. The studies of this period in English, French and German are so numerous, and display, as a rule, such a workmanlike attention to detail, that it seems preferable in the present context not to embark on yet another recapitulation, but to summarize and interpret the material available.[2]

According to Marjorie Nicolson, "*Paradise Lost* and [Thomas Burnet's] *Sacred Theory of the Earth* were the two most widely read theodicies of the earlier eighteenth century."[3] The authors of these works had in common a tendency to imagine and describe "the transfer of vastness from God to interstellar space, then to terrestrial mountains."[4] Thomas Weiskel has plausibly argued that this tendency occurred in "response to the darker implications of Locke's psychology."

> If the only route to the intellect lies through the senses, belief in a supernatural Being finds itself insecure. God had to be saved, even if He had to marry the world of appearances. And so, in the natural sublime, He did. . . . The emotions traditionally religious were displaced from the Deity and became associated first with the immensity of space and secondarily with the natural phenomena (oceans, mountains) which seemed to approach that immensity.[5]

But the poetic benefits that flowed from this displacement of religious feeling were not so intoxicating in every quarter as to prevent certain critics from lamenting the fact that, in "marrying the world of appearances," God had suffered a demotion. How otherwise can the new taste for horror be explained? If God had retained all his power in transit, those eighteenth-century witnesses of avalanches and thunderstorms would not have been affected with "pleasant trembling,"[6] but with more violent symptoms of terror. Their response to the natural signs of God's wrath would not have been less desperate, less unlike an aesthetic response, than that of Jonathan Edwards's parishioners to his descriptions of hellfire.[7] As Weiskel says, "if the danger is real we turn and flee, without pausing for our sublime moment."[8] But if God's displeasure has ceased to pose a threat to one's soul, and has taken instead the form of a natural spectacle, it loses much of its strength as a deterrent from flouting his law. The strongest sensations, such as horror, can be immoderately enjoyed.

This was the view of Burke, whose theory of the sublime is distinguished by "its determined exclusiveness. He is at pains to reduce the traditional occasions of the sublime to the motive of terror."[9] Between that extreme, however, and the moral chastity of Johnson, there are many intermediate positions. John Dennis, for one, recognized that objects "likely to hurt" us produce terror, but that the "Ideas of those objects" produce "Enthusiastick Terror."[10] In this he anticipates Burke, who, as A. C. Bradley noted, "changed the character of fear by removing the immediate threat of danger so that the 'astonishment' that fills the mind is delighful."[11] Unlike Burke, however, Dennis sanctifies his delight in terrible ideas by regarding them as the proofs that God is great.

> Gods, Daemons, Hell, Spirits and Souls of Men, Miracles, Prodigies, Enchantments, Witchcraft, Thunder, Tempests, raging Seas, Inundations, Torrents, Earthquakes, Volcanoes, Monsters, Serpents, Lions, Tygers, Fire, War, Pestilence, Famine, etc. [are ideas which] will be found to be the more terrible, as they have the more of religion in them.[12]

Johnson might well have upbraided John Dennis with bad faith on the evidence of this passage, had his creed not enjoined him to refrain from throwing the first stone. For how is it possible simultaneously to affirm the reality of an invisible God, and take pleasure in the thought of His wrath? Dennis's careful distinction between terrible objects, which are not a source of pleasure, and the ideas of those objects, which are, is inadmissible from Johnson's point of view, because it implies that the fate reserved by God for sensualists—a fate of which we can only form an idea—is unreal. Johnson would have questioned the sincerity of Dennis's belief that nothing is "more terrible than the Idea of an angry God,"[13] since that belief prompts him not to fast and pray and contemplate his sins in silence, but to rave about "Gods, Daemons, Hell, Spirits," etc. The simplicity of Dennis's regret, however, "that by divesting itself of Religion, [modern poetry] is fallen from its Dignity, and its original Nature and Excellence,"[14] belies such an imputation; and we had better avoid the charge of invidiousness by concluding merely, that Dennis, unlike Johnson, seems to have belonged to the class of "almost all persons, who . . . are quite free from uneasiness as to their prospects in another world, and never for a moment seem to think themselves in any real danger of eternal punishment."[15] This attitude, according to J. S Mill, "contributed much to the downfall of the old religions."[16] It is an attitude which explains the blatant sensationalism and amorality of later theories of the sublime; but one which also, by 1867, had infused sufficient skepticism into the intellectual climate of Europe to enable Mallarmé to declare, that he had no more use for "ce vieux et méchant plumage . . . Dieu."[17] The force of his scorn may be gauged by his treatment of the metaphor of the wing, represented metonymically here as a "plumage." The broken or aged wing is a recurrent symbol in Mallarmé's writings,[18] constituting the negative half of "an opposition easily polarized—'lofty flight' versus 'lamed wing.' "[19] The notion of "proud" or "highest flight" originates with Longinus, and possesses in common with other groups of images that have attached themselves to the sublime in every age, the property of suggesting the subject's capacity to assume a superior position with respect to an object of nature. This movement is central to the sublime experience, as we shall see in chapter nine. For the present it is enough to observe, that according to Mallarmé's metaphor, God, as an engine of flight, is too infirm to lift the subject to the necessary height, and too distasteful (*méchant*) to be cherished as an object of devotion.

Other theorists of the eighteenth century were prepared to enlarge the scope of God's intercourse with the world, and to celebrate his presence in situations that would have seemed morally neutral, or doubtful, or reprehensible, to Johnson. In his *Essay on Taste* of 1759, for example, Alexander Gerard accounted for his delight in the villains of Shakespearean tragedy by observing, that "a perfect imitation of characters morally evil, can make us dwell with pleasure on them, notwithstanding the uneasy sentiments of disapprobation and abhorrence which they excite."[20] This view, which posits the independence of rectitude and artistic quality, was advanced by many artists of the mid- and late-nineteenth century; but it is surprising to find the didactic intention in art denounced as early as 1805 by Richard Payne Knight in his *Analytical Inquiry into the Principles of Taste.* Knight supports Gerard and attacks his contemporary Archibald Alison[21] by maintaining, that our delight in the masterful depiction of evil characters should not be confused with whatever heightened appreciation of virtue the behavior of such characters may enable us to gain. William Hazlitt made the same point in stronger language when he rejected the casuistry that had reduced Milton's Satan to a foil for the glory of God.[22] Literary creations that "increase the reader's sense of power" are bound to engage his sympathy, Hazlitt argued, whether they are edifying or not. The appeal of Hazlitt's own vigorous writings—an appeal that owes nothing to charity, humility, or any other Christian virtue except compassion—seems to attest the truth of his view; but there is also reason to believe that his opponent Alison was inspired by a genuine loathing of evil, and not by the spirit of sanctimony, when he devised the explanation that provided him with a creditable motive for damnable sympathies. This reason is, that the determination to find a proof of God's omnipotence in the very potency of evil was not limited, in the eighteenth century, to discussions of literary characters like Satan and Iago, but extended to situations in which ethics applied only remotely, or not at all. "The great emptiness [of space] itself," Ernest Tuveson observes, "[was] a reassurance and not a terror, for it [was] the guarantee of a divine Mind that sustain[ed] order in the frightful multiplicity and impersonality of the cosmos."[23] Such an interpretation of the natural world cannot be dismissed as an attempt to remove the taint of sinfulness that otherwise would have spoiled the eighteenth-century aesthete's enjoyment of "great emptiness." Real fear must have prompted it. For how can one's reactions to the natural world have a bearing on the fate of one's soul? Personal salvation does not depend, in any Christian doctrine, on whether one delights in "that deep romantic Chasm," or shrinks from "le silence éternel de ces espaces infinis."[24]

To discriminate in finer detail, or at greater length, between the theories of the sublime advanced by Dennis, Alison, Knight and Gerard, would be to give the impression that these authors are remarkable rather for the points on which they differ, than for those on which they agree. But in their common attempt to reconcile the ungodly delight afforded by tremendous natural spectacles and by evil characters artfully drawn, with the exigencies of their belief in a stern and otherworldly religion, Dennis, Alison, Knight and Gerard are united. To avoid the necessity of repudiating the article of faith which asserted God's hostility to the world of appearances, they were forced to resort to the dubious paradoxes described above—paradoxes which had not yet been softened into Keats's "holiness of the Heart's affections,"[25] or into the attitude suggested by the following passage from *Modern Painters:*

> Although there was no definite religious sentiment mingled with it, there was a continual perception of Sanctity in the whole of nature, from the slightest thing to the vastest;—an instinctive awe, mixed with delight.[26]

This sort of easygoing pantheism was not available to the troubled proponents of the eighteenth-century religious sublime. Their God customarily revealed himself by giving signs that he was displeased: the "Tempests, raging Seas, Inundations" and other scourges of Dennis's list. Yet, as we have seen, some degree of religious skepticism must have been present in order for the "Ideas of terrible objects" to have been thought sublime, rather than merely terrible. Belief in God requires that one love and fear an idea more than any object. The very fact that, in the period under review, God should have adopted only fearsome avatars—that, in representing him as a fiction, Dennis and the others should have dwelt exclusively on his terible side—is a sign that, even for the most freethinking among them, such fictions still bore the character of blasphemy. Burke, for example, having observed that we take "no small delight . . . in the real misfortunes" of our fellow creatures, tries to palliate the moral blame attaching to such delight by inventing a theological law: "as our Creator has designed that we should be united by the bond of sympathy, he has strengthened that bond by a proportionable delight; and there most where our sympathy is most wanted,—in the distresses of others."[27] Hence the paradox: "We delight in seeing things, which so far from doing, our heartiest wishes would be to see redressed."[28] The fallacious logic of this argument is betrayed by the duplication of the verb "to see": the paradox has an appearance of cogency which arises from the imprecision of its terms.[29] The question of truth or error is less interesting here, however, than the fact that a disciple of Locke, like Locke himself, should have tried to justify his empirical observations on religious grounds; going so far, in the present case, as to "discover" a moral sanction for *Schadenfreude*.

Our survey of the religious sublime points to a conclusion which Thomas Weiskel has already drawn: "in the history of literary consciousness the sublime revives as God withdraws from an immediate participation in the experience of man."[30] We have seen how the immediacy of God in Samuel Johnson's spiritual life made him forego the attempt to convey the ideal by literary means. "Contemplative piety," according to him, "cannot be poetical. Man . . . is already in a higher state than poetry can confer."[31] Many of his contemporaries,[32] however, believed with John Dennis that "religion [is] the true wellspring of great poetry."[33] This belief led them to carry out a profane transaction: they sought to make the world more numinous and their poetry more sublime by violating the ideality of God.

Chapter Six

Ironic and enthusiastic attitudes to the ideal: to speak of it or not? Irony of Mallarmé's attitude. His reluctance to name the ideal compared with Johnson's. Faith, a form of enthusiasm, and its literary product, the Word. Mallarmé's hopes of doing justice to the ideal in words.

Two principles of central importance to our thesis must now be named: the principles of *irony* and *enthusiasm.* It was the operation of the second of these (from the Greek *enthousiazein,* "to be inspired or possessed by the god")[1] that enabled John Dennis to conflate God and the world, the ideal and the real. Had his attitude been more ironic than enthusiastic, the conflation would have seemed a confusion to him, as it did to Johnson and to Mallarmé. In a moment we shall consider how irony and enthusiasm affect the character of the literary work. But first, let us conclude our discussion of the religious sublime by answering the question whether Mallarmé himself ever said anything about the relation of God and man to the sublime.

He did. In a letter of 1866 to Henri Cazalis he wrote:

> Oui, *je le sais,* nous ne sommes que de vaines formes de la matière, mais bien sublimes pour avoir inventé Dieu et notre

> âme. Si sublimes, mon ami! que je veux me donner ce spectacle de la matière, ayant conscience d'être et, cependant, s'élançant forcénément dans le Rêve qu'elle sait n'être pas, chantant l'Ame et toutes les divines impressions pareilles qui se sont amassées en nous depuis les premiers âges et proclamant, devant le Rien qui est la vérité, ces glorieux mensonges![2]

This passage is thoroughly informed with the spirit of irony. The word "cependant" expresses by itself the sense of contradiction, and therefore stands as the fulcrum of the passage, on either side of which the other parts of speech may be grouped: "*je le sais*" with its objective clause versus "je veux me donner ce spectacle"; "vaines formes de la matière" versus "bien sublimes"; "inventé" versus "Dieu et notre âme"; "ayant conscience d'être" versus "s'élançant forcénément dans le Rêve" and the other enthusiastic gerunds; those gerunds versus their nonexistent objects; "le Rien" versus "la vérité"; "glorieux" versus "mensonges."[3] The gist of the opposition is contained in the first of these pairs, *je sais* and *je veux*; but the opposition is not static; the two camps do not cancel each other out. Instead, an endless dialectic between knowledge and desire is described: one knows that one exists, that one is a form of matter (contradiction: to know that one exists makes one something more than a form of matter, since knowledge is not material); one desires the ideal which, being immaterial, does not exist (contradiction: one desires that which does not exist); one knows that one cannot have what does not exist, yet one desires what one cannot have (since it is only what one cannot have that remains the object which desire cannot extinguish itself by reaching). The confusion in this account is unavoidable: it arises from the necessity of describing the ideal, which is beyond time and is not a thing, in sentences that unroll temporally from noun to noun. To say, for example, that Mallarmé identifies the sublime in our knowledge that we desire what we know we cannot have, is wrong. It is not the knowledge that is sublime, or the desire, but (to pursue our notion of a dialectic) the synthesis that emerges from the chastening influence of knowledge on desire, and the invigorating influence of desire on knowledge. Pleasure should supplement the reader's confusion, however, since that confusion is a sign that his desire for knowledge—his desire to comprehend the ideal—has not been satisfied: there is still something left to be desired. We are spared the disaster, we are denied the fulfillment of comprehending the ideal—a disaster and fulfillment that only death can inflict and bestow. But we are sublime in our capacity to feel again an inkling of what we have just realized we cannot comprehend.

Perhaps the most notable feature of this text, however, is the italicization of the words "je le sais." By this means the text implies that the ironical view of man's place in creation which it describes is to be taken as a profession of faith. This implication of course adds another layer of irony to the text; but it also furnishes the element of enthusiasm without which, as we shall see, the sublime experience cannot be produced. In the study of specific texts to be conducted in part two, we shall investigate the author's characteristic procedure of converting the necessary irony of his perceptions into a principle of (aesthetic) faith. Although his practice of his art was characterized by a thoroughgoing irony, the art itself he conceived as a religion. To have said this much, however, is greatly to have anticipated our argument.

Here we might make a further distinction between the statement that the ideal does not exist and the statement that it exists ideally, i.e. that it exists without form. But in either case, the problem of devising a satisfactory literary treatment of the ideal remains the same. Granted that the ideal does not exist (or exists without form), nevertheless, it is the property of language to describe. When the subject of discourse is the ideal, therefore, language must be used in a negative way: "il faut encore *dire* ce qu'on *nie*" (as Michael Riffaterre has said). Mallarmé was among the first to recognize the implications of this fact. It is the poet's duty, he believed, to write about the ideal; yet, in making sense of his subject, the poet fails. (Precisely insofar as a poem is comprehensible, it fails to render the ideal.)[4] Only by eluding the reader's understanding, by piquing yet baffling his curiosity, does the poet remain faithful to the ideal. Only by demonstrating that his poem has not attained its object—that it cannot help but fail to attain its object—and by inducing the reader to regard this demonstration, not as a cause for despair, but as a proof that our ability to see through the illusion of success makes us "bien sublimes"—that every disenchantment brings us momentarily closer to a goal which we can only approach asymptotically—only in this demonstration, in the execution of this bitter and exalting task, does the poet answer the vocation which emanates from within himself, and which leads him nowhere but to the grave. In part two of this study we shall show how Mallarmé's attempt to "effacer toute ligne de démarcation entre la poésie lyrique et le récit de sa genèse" (as Eric Gans has called it)[5] bears out the truth of Emerson's remark, that "the sublime [is] felt in an analysis as well as in a creation."[6]

The God in whose existence Johnson faithfully believed, is an invention according to Mallarmé. But it is not surprising that the two writers' disagreement on a matter so nearly absolute as this—whether to award the title of Final Cause to God or to man—should have produced so little difference in their answers to the practical question: what is the proper literary treatment of the ideal? Both of them recommended that it not be named. The best-known enunciation of this view in Mallarmé occurs in the "Réponse à une enquête de Jules Huret": "Nommer un objet, c'est supprimer les trois quarts de la jouissance du poème."[7] This ban does not apply only to objects, but *a fortiori* to the ideal, which suffers a worse degradation in being coined and reduced to a grubby counter in the traffic of words.[8] But where Mallarmé's purpose in omitting to name the ideal is aesthetic, Johnson's is instrumental: the ideal is not empowered to save Mallarmé's soul; God may save Johnson's. (The two motivations exactly correspond to Kant's *Zweck* and *Zweckmässigkeit ohne Zweck*.) The silence which Mallarmé volunteered, was extorted from Johnson. Pure logic prompted the Frenchman, once his thought had "thought itself through,"[9] to deny himself the act which Johnson's religion defined as blasphemy—viz., the uttering of the Tetragrammaton. For through the mouthpiece of Rasselas, Johnson refers to God as "the Being whom I fear to name."[10]

It is this recognition of the necessity for silence concerning the ideal that links Mallarmé's thought to that of Johnson and to the ancient stages of the sublime tradition. But the opinion held by a given writer about the relative literary values of speech and silence seems always to be formed in accordance with his decision to believe or disbelieve in the reality and attainability of the ideal. The triumph of enthusiasm over irony is here more precisely the triumph of faith over disbelief. Faith transforms the ideal into God, who directly governs and participates in the world of appearances. The literary consequence of this transformation is a Word more perfect, more potent, more sublime than silence—the *logos* that figures as often as anyone cites scripture to illustrate his conception of sublimity. Coleridge, for example, quotes Hebrews xii. 18–22: after the tempest comes "the voice of words; which voice they that heard entreated that the word should not be spoken to them any more."[11] Hegel quotes Psalm 104; Longinus the first lines of Genesis. In describing the Word as a literary consequence of faith, we have chosen our adjective advisedly; for although the Word has what might be called a superliterary importance in Jewish and Christian doctrine (being the "actively expressed, creative, and revelatory thought and will of God")[12] it is nonetheless clearly distinguished from God himself. Therefore the critic, whether he professes to be a servant of God or an atheist, is not guilty of apostasy if he ascribes great power to the Word at one point in his writings, and elsewhere denies that it is superior to silence. Longinus quotes Genesis, to be sure; but he also says that the silence of Ajax in Book XI of the *Odyssey* is "more sublime than any words."[13] By affirming the supremacy of the Word in the first example, and that of silence in the second, Longinus does not impugn his own good faith. He merely exchanges one set of literary assumptions for another. The ghost of Ajax says nothing—that is, leaves everything unsaid. No disappointing utterance prevents the reader from reading as much "nobility of mind" into that silence as he has imagination to conceive; but the extent to which he does so, the extent to which he finds the silence of Ajax sublime, depends on how deeply he has participated in the spirit of the epic—on how enthusiastically he has taken to heart the conventions that make Ajax a hero. Likewise the sublimity of the passages from Genesis is only available to the reader who, like Longinus, has accepted for the time being the premise, that God's Word cannot disappoint, because *infinite* power is not diminished by the act of taking form. Mallarmé, coincidentally, was as flexible as Longinus in this matter. The very obliquity of his art makes it clear that he understood the superiority of silence to speech—for what is obliquity, after all, but applied silence? On the other hand, his long-standing intention to write the ultimate Book, the "Orphic explanation of the earth,"[14] suggests that he entertained the possibility of devising an unimprovable form of words which would yield nothing to silence in point of mystery and inscrutability;—that he wished to frame the utterance which no regret for the perfect silence it destroyed would succeed.[15]

A worthwhile study might be undertaken by a critic of Mallarmé's poetry who is also a competent biblical scholar, comparing the literary techniques employed in both cases to create respect and desire for the ideal. The theological concept of "veiled discourse," based on Christ's practice of speaking in parables, can be made out behind the determination of all the Symbolist poets "to express," as Rémy de Gourmont put it, "only the second term of a comparison."[16] In general, however, the language and character of late-nineteenth-century literature support no other conclusion than that the attempt to demonstrate a real biblical influence is far-fetched. The appeal of Catholicism for Huysmans, for example, appears to have been primarily of an aesthetic order, as it was for Frederick Rolfe and the other contemporaries of Mallarmé who exploited the potential of the Mass for creating a vaguely spiritual atmosphere. Mallarmé alone of his generation invented a personal grammar which, highly compressed yet reposeful, recalls the paratactic quality of Hebrew,[17] and which, moreover, serves the same purpose of sequestering an unspeakable ideal.[18]

Chapter Seven

Tendency of enthusiasts to name things without reflecting that the words are not the things themselves. Enthusiasm alone does not confer literary distinction (John Dennis). No one rhetorical figure specially suited for the expression of enthusiasm. Enthusiasm and hyperbole. Longinus's and the Romantics' attitudes to hyperbole contrasted.

We are bound to increase our understanding of the nature of irony if we turn our attention for a moment to the principle which opposes it, and consider the effect of enthusiasm on the production of the literary text. No one, it is safe to say, has ever been more completely under the empire of that principle than John Dennis; and our discussion of enthusiasm may as well begin with some further remarks on the passage from his *Grounds of Criticism* quoted in chapter five. This passage has been singled out by several modern critics as an example of "debased Longinianism,"[1] by which they presumably mean that it offers a bad recipe for concocting the rhetorical sublime. The recipe seems bad because it lacks astringency. There is no ingredient to cut the author's enthusiastic belief, that by naming those prodigies of nature he will make us feel their sublimity. He is so taken with the ideas of the things for which his words stand as to forget the dinginess and intractability of the words themselves. The traces of order in his list are feeble, and suggest that the process of association which led him to put, for instance, "Fire" after "Tyger," was not under his control. Such strictures as these will only be heard from readers who cannot bring themselves to pump up the words with enthusiasm, as Dennis does. The entire difference between this state of mind and that of his detractors Pope and Gay is made clear at the end of the passage. He observes that the elements in his list "will be found to be the more terrible, as they have the more of religion in them." The word "religion," however, is merely an enthusiastic substitute for the neutral word "enthusiasm": it signifies that enthusiasm has been placed beyond the reach of irony—or rather, that irony is just a fair name for blasphemy. By evaluating literature according to the standard of devotional excellence, Dennis falls into the error which Johnson and Mallarmé avoided. Enthusiasm is a quality of which one cannot have too much in the religious life. When sealed off from doubt and directed at a particular object, it is indistinguishable from faith. But *literary* immortality is not procured with enthusiasm alone. One fails to conceive of a mimesis or arrangement of symbols completely lacking in irony, for which the claim of artistic distinction can plausibly be made. This is to say that before the artist can "evaporate the disagreeables" (in Keats's phrase) he must be able to recognize them. If enthusiasm were the sole criterion of literary composition, texts would have no form: no internal form (since there would be no standard by which to establish a relative order of importance among the elements of the text) and no total form (since there would be no reason to cease to include new elements in the catalogue of indiscriminate approval). The artist must therefore play the *eiron* to his own creative *alazon* if he is to fashion an enduring artifact, or even an artifact that endures only long enough to be recognized as such before it is dismissed or forgotten. Yet the presence of irony can be drastically reduced in proportion to that of enthusiasm. What are the consequences of such a reduction?

It requires no very comprehensive survey of enthusiastic literature to show, that the use of a given rhetorical figure is not exclusively reserved for the purpose of creating enthusiasm, and what is less obvious, that certain figures are not better suited than their opposites to accomplishing that end. Longinus discourages the use of conjunctions, for example, as tending to "hamper" and "tone down" enthusiasm, and quotes from the *Odyssey* to illustrate how "force in thrusting together" should be applied.[2] Yet the author of the following passage conveys his enthusiasm by multiplying the number of conjunctions, annexing a new strength to his subject with every copulative:

> Alike in the highest regions of speculation and in the smaller practical concerns of daily life, her mind was the same perfect instrument, piercing to the very heart and marrow of the matter. . . . The same exactness and rapidity of operation, pervading as it did her sensitive as well as her mental faculties, would, with her gifts of feeling and imagination, have fitted her to be a consummate artist, as her fiery and tender soul and her vigorous eloquence would certainly have made her a great orator, and her profound knowledge of human nature and discernment and sagacity in practical life, would . . . have made her eminent among the rulers of mankind.[3]

Longinus elsewhere asserts that we are more likely to be "carried away by the enthusiasm of the speaker" who does not "soften the effect" of his metaphors by introducing them with some word or phrase of comparison.[4] But the enthusiasm excited by the lyrics of popular songs suggests that, on the contrary, it may not be the actual terms of a comparison, or the transition from one term to the next, so much as the mere announcement of the approach of the second term conveyed by the word "like," that moves us; for the terms themselves are usually hackneyed, but the word "like" has still the power of a portent,[5] which it exerts the more effectively as the disappointment occasioned by the arrival of the second term is reduced by the distraction of the music, and the evil which attends the use of the portent as a literary device—its tendency to seem, in retrospect,[6] to have been too portentous—is avoided. Again, one critic,[7] having noticed that Longinus draws many of his examples of high-pitched enthusiasm from the category of brief outbursts, wrongly declares that according to Longinus, enthusiasm can only be sustained for the length of such an outburst—a declaration which Longinus's remarks on the suitability of the periodic sentence as a vehicle for enthusiasm permit us to discount.[8] (That Mallarmé agreed with Longinus on this point is made clear by the following excerpt from "Quant au Livre": "Pourquoi—un jet de grandeur, de pensée ou d'émoi, considérable, phrase poursuivie, en gros caractère, une ligne par page à emplacement gradué, ne maintiendrait-il le lecteur en haleine. la durée du livre, avec appel à sa *puissance d'enthousiasme*.")[9] And even if we give up the attempt to single out a rhetorical figure specially favored by enthusiastic writers, and try instead to show that enthusiasm has been consistently identified with some large order of imagery or particular cluster of themes, we shall have no better results, inasmuch as we cannot determine the allegiance of enthusiasm even in so basic a thematic conflict as the one between light and dark, and must acknowledge, for every place in *Peri Hupsous* where "enthusiasm" is coupled with words like "brilliance" and "effluence,"[10] a passage in Burke's *Inquiry* where the author repeats his settled conviction, that "clarity is the enemy of enthusiasm."[11] This universal frustration of our attempts to establish that some quarter of the repertoire of figures holds a notable affinity for enthusiasm, bears in upon us the conclusion, that enthusiasm does not affect "les structures du langage littéraire" in any predictable way, but rather "celles de l'intention créatrice" (as Eric Gans has called them);[12] that it nourishes, more precisely, the hyperbolic intention.[13]

We must be on guard against the error, which our sympathy with the aims and admiration for the achievements of the Romantics make us liable to commit, of supposing that, since the purpose of hyperbole is to exalt its subject towards the ideal, it is by itself a sufficient means of producing the sublime experience. In fact, as our discussion of the passage from Mallarmé in chapter six was meant to show, the presence of irony is required as a complement or corrective to hyperbole, in order for justice to be done to the ideal. We know that the ideal cannot be attained; and we recognize in hyperbole the discharge of enthusiasm. Whatever else it may be, therefore, the subject of hyperbole is never the ideal: for how can we "overshoot" what we cannot even reach? Yet it is the nature of hyperbole to induce us to forget this fact: that it does not describe the state of a thing, but rather what it would wish the thing to be. It succeeds by passing off a lie on the reader; by injecting so heady a dose of idealism into his fare, that the resistance of his faculties is overcome, and he gives himself up to the enjoyment of the illusion. Longinus understood this very well. He knew that in using an hyperbole, the orator departs from "reality and truth,"[14] and that if the departure is not put across with plenty of contagious enthusiasm, it will be seen for what it is. But the Romantics did not, on the whole, understand. They evidently believed, or wished to believe, in the letter of their hyperbole. Hazlitt's late essay on "The Ideal," for example, "makes clear his belief that any notion of perfection beyond 'the highest conceivable degree of any quality or excellence diffused over the whole of an object . . . is a word without meaning—a thing in the clouds.' "[15] For Coleridge, "the loftiest of all possible intuitions is of 'supremacy of being as it is.' "

> Hast thou ever raised thy mind to the consideration of existence, in and by itself, as the mere act of existing? Has thou ever said to thyself thoughtfully: It is! [If so,] thou wilt have felt the presence of a mystery, which must have fixed thy spirit in awe and in wonder.[16]

Keats, too, located the "ordered permanence of essence [in] the chaos of sensation."[17] But the plainest, baldest profession of the doctrine that the ideal is fully present in the real, occurs in Burke's chapter on "Infinity," which has been ably summed up as follows: "By infinity, Burke means anything that, by virtue of its size, cannot be encompassed by *the eye* and is, therefore, *thought* to be infinite."[18] The ironical retort to this—that if, like Burke, we start thinking with our eyes, we shall soon, like him, begin to see things—belongs to the class of barbed comments whose function is to "dégonfler la fausse sublimité" (as Vladimir Jankélévitch described it).[19] Before turning to that aspect of the matter, however, we should conclude the present section of our argument by repeating, that when a writer makes use of hyperbole, he expends his enthusiasm on something less than the ideal. It is no accident that the generation of writers for whom, as M. H. Abrams said, "the question of the ideal in poetry . . . lost the special position it had held in earlier theory,"[20] should also have been a generation so frequently incapable of distinguishing hyperbole from truth.

Chapter Eight

Enthusiasm vulnerable to irony. Enthusiasm may be supplied by reader as well as writer. Important facts a defense of enthusiasm against irony. Enthusiasm disguises hyperbole's "departure from truth". Predominance of irony in modern attitude. Deceptive power of hyperbole not felt by modern critics. Hyperbole an exception to rule of literariness.

No doubt because, in a sober estimation, we recognize that our own chances of attaining the sublime are small, we tend to think pretentious, and consequently, ridiculous, the efforts of other persons to attain it, when those efforts fail conspicuously, or all but succeed. This danger was present to Longinus's mind, and induced him, as we have argued, not to ascend in his enthusiasm beyond a height at which the ordinary members of his audience could still follow him. Even he, who admitted the possibility of reaching a sublime level of discourse without the assistance of strong emotion, was aware that the same "factors are the foundation and origin, not only of success but also of its opposite."[1] Everything we have read about the eighteenth- and nineteenth-century conceptions of the sublime confirms, however, that the artist's susceptibility to ridicule increases in the degree to which he relies on enthusiasm as the "factor of success." If he does not inspire confidence on other grounds, his invitation to share in his enthusiasm will not be taken up—unless, indeed, his audience brings to the encounter a superabundance of ready enthusiasm of its own. For if it is true that one must, at one extreme, adopt the airlessly high standards of Samuel Johnson in order to concur in his denunciation of the *Conquest of Granada* as an "approach to the precipice of absurdity," and to understand how he can have detected too strong and admixture of "the ridiculous . . . with the astonishing" in that magnificent play,[2] it is no less true that readers were not wanting to find great merit in what Thomas De Quincey called the "absurd pamphlets" of John Dennis,[3] and to derive their experience of sublimity from a source which De Quincey could not enjoy. We should hesitate to conclude that any reader's experience of sublimity is less genuine than De Quincey's or Johnson's, merely because he is less fastidious than they. The point to be made is rather, that the "tension of emotional context"[4] required by Longinus and others as a precondition for the use of hyperbole, can be generated by the passive, as well as by the active party in a communication. An enthusiastic audience can breathe life into the matter of a dull or ill-conducted speech.[5] René Bary, a seventeenth-century French critic, for example, observed that in the sublime style "l'on doit enchérir sur les mots"; "au lieu de dire: ce que je vous présente est un cercle, l'on doit dire: la chose dont je vous entretiens, est une surface qui est de tous côtés également distante de son centre."[6] Now most readers will agree with Jules Brody that this improvement on the *genus humile* has only an absurd pretention to being considered sublime. Like him they will be unable to supply the enthusiasm which clearly did not possess the author. Yet it is possible to imagine the case of a fanatical geometrist with a taste for unmotivated paraphrase, to whom the passage might represent the last word in sublimity.

We could not wish for a more conclusive proof of our

argument, that enthusiasm not only inspires hyperbole but disguises its divergence from "reality and truth," than we have in the circumstance that Longinus, who regarded hyperbole dispassionately and saw it for a lie, set great store by the facts upon which it must operate, while the Romantics did not.[7] A speaker who refers to matters of compelling interest or vital consequence to his audience, is doubly fortunate in his subject: for, on the one hand, he need not exaggerate its importance at all, being called on merely to rise to an occasion already sufficiently high, and which requires that he risk nothing more fanciful than an accurate and objective treatment; and, on the other, he can hardly exaggerate its importance too much, since his audience will certainly applaud the most enthusiastic claims and superlative comparisons made on their own behalf. The attempted deception of hyperbole is more likely to fail when the facts do not warrant, in the judgment of the intended dupes, the enthusiasm solicited for them. Then the audience, suspecting that the transport in which the speaker appears to be rapt is not genuine, since they cannot share it, will come to regard him as tending either towards the condition of the lunatic or the charlatan—unless, of course, his intention is satirical, satire being, as Longinus remarked, the deliberate "exaggeration of pettiness."[8] But the power of enthusiasm to cast itself, as well as mean or trifling objects, in an enthusiastic light, is suggested by the unqualified form of Hazlitt's affirmation, that the "intensity of the feeling makes up for the disproportion of the objects."[9] We have only to recall Wordsworth's raptures over the "sublime" vigil of a starving dog by the side of his dead master,[10] or Coleridge's amazing encomium of the "Llama's dung-pellet" quoted in chapter one, to extinguish whatever doubt still remains, that the Romantics were thoroughly steeped in the spirit of enthusiasm.

Not only the real and the ideal, then, but the speaker and his audience are momentarily united by the tension of hyperbole. Perhaps we have looked at the second of these unions too ironically, and ought not to have stood so far to one side. In describing the acceptors of hyperbole as dupes, for example, we imputed a dishonest intention to the speaker, where we might with more truth have referred to a joint delusion. We have conceived of the literary encounter as taking place in a public arena, and of the audience as being predisposed to jump down the speaker's throat. Like the *eiron* of Socratic dialogue we have always kept in view the "distance du moi aux objets et distance d'objet à objet"; we have not felt much of the *alazon*'s "urgence vitale."[11] We have borne out the dismal truth of Thomas Weiskel's saying, that modern critics "have long since been too ironic for the . . . Romantic sublime."[12] When Ruskin tops off his description of the Alban Mount[13] by comparing the "masses of entangled and tall foliage" to "the curtains of God's tabernacle," we regret that he has gone (as we think) too far, for we lack the faith to endorse his hyperbole. When Scott or Mrs. Radcliffe tells us, as they usually do,[14] that the scene they have just described is "Romantic" or "sublime," we wish they had resisted the impulse to "souligner lourdement."[15] We find more truth in the organic metropolis of *Ulysses* than in Plato's divine metaphors for the human body.[16] Like the second speaker in the following exchange from one of Maurice Dekobra's novels, we require that the tenor of hyperbole should not sag beneath its load:

> —Ne trouvez-vous pas que Lady Diana Wynham a eu une idée sublime en me suggérant de faire des documentaires sur les alliés de la Croisade démocratique?
> —L'idée est plus que sublime, chef. Elle n'est même pas mal du tout.[17]

It might be objected that any literary text lays itself open to ironic deflation by purporting to mean something other than what it says. But if we have been right to identify in hyperbole the trace of a movement towards the ideal, and right to maintain that, as the natural expression of enthusiasm, it was peculiarly fitted to encourage the Romantics in their practice of throwing themselves on the reader's sympathy, then we are also right to insist that it should not be regarded primarily as a symptom of literariness. For unlike every other means of adding a formal significance to discourse, the use of hyperbole is intended to take us, not just *away* from the literal, but *to* the ideal. It is not merely a gesture but a displacement. Unlike the stylistic facts of a text, which require to be interpreted as departures from the norm of literal communication (i.e. as variations or comments upon the message conveyed by the linguistic facts of the text), the structure of hyperbole requires the reader to credit unreal assertions as literal truth. In other words, hyperbole does not function by affording the reader an appreciation of the difference between what is stressed and what is expressed, but by blinding him to that difference.

Let us turn for a proof of this to the works of Christopher Marlowe, "the first English writer," according to Swinburne, "whose powers can be called sublime."[18] Marlovian hyperbole consists in ascribing to a human subject a greater degree of some virtue than the divine or mythical paragon of that virtue possessed—as in:

> Oh, thou art fairer than the Evening air
> Clad in the beauty of a thousand stars!
> Brighter art thou than flaming Jupiter,
> When he appear'd to hapless Semele:
> More lovely than the monarch of the sky,
> In wanton Arethusa's azur'd arms. . . .[19]

The tenor is impossibly asserted to be greater than the vehicle—impossibly, that is, if we allow ourselves to overlook the presence on stage of an actor to whom these lines are addressed. This liberty will not seem excessive when we recall that Marlowe uses the same device throughout his non-dramatic poetry, although it is certainly one of his intentions here to establish the peerlessness in the flesh of his Helen, by setting her before us in "the brittle splendour of erotic vision."[20] The nature of hyperbole will appear more clearly once the lines are disencumbered of their perishable referent. Then the reader will observe that he has not experienced the metaphors in the usual way. His imagination has not been shuttled between the tenor "thou" and the several vehicles, but boosted onto each vehicle in order to look beyond it. He has been told that Helen is "fairer," "brighter" and "more lovely" than the superlative embodiments of those qualities; he cannot therefore be content to compare her to them, but must put forth his own resources in an effort to outdo the speaker. In this he will certainly fail, not because his powers are inferior to Marlowe's, but because new images are constantly forthcoming from the "poet of torrential imagination,"[21] and so long as he does not lay aside the book, the reader is obliged to acquiesce in the tyranny of the text. Since each vehicle is not the limit of a comparison, but only the intermediate stage in an unfinished journey, we do not reflect that it is after all something of a disappointment, because we have reserved the full measure of our enthusiasm for what is yet to come. The Evening air, Jupiter and Arethusa are proposed as (at best) second-bests; they cannot cloy, because they are not meant to satisfy. Our potential wish to disprize the poet's conceptions is not excited, because he does not claim too much for them. On the contrary, he encourages us to surpass them if we can; a maneuver which serves his purpose very well, by inclining us to admire *en passant* the efforts of so generous an ally. In this enthusiastic state we have no sense that the vehicle of Marlovian metaphor obstructs the career of our imagination, shot through as the former appears to be with the glamour of an unseen ideal.

We have been arguing that the reader made credulous by the fumes of enthusiasm will mistake for the genuine article the mere simulacrum of the ideal placed within his grasp by hyperbole. Now if our only evidence in support of this view were contained in the brief anatomy of that figure just conducted, we should probably suppose that we had fallen into some error. For it is a view which contemporary theorists strongly deny. Fontanier, for one, has written that "L'hyperbole augmente . . . les choses avec excès . . . dans la vue, non de tromper, mais d'amener à la vérité même, et de fixer, par ce qu'elle dit d'incroyable, ce qu'il faut réellement croire."[22] Eric Gans similarly argues that "Ce qui crée la 'réflexivité' particulière de l'hyperbole, c'est que l'esprit, dans l'acte de la lecture, ne puisse saisir le sens des mots qu'à partir d'un *jugement* sur leur référent. L'hyperbole ne comporte pas . . . un transfert de sens, mais un arrêt du bon sens sur le degré auquel il faut entendre son contenu sémantique."[23]—But is it not rather the ironic than the hyperbolic intention that prompts us to make such a judgment? Our common sense did not balk as we read the lines from *Faustus*, nor would it have done if we had not first dismissed the referent. When the tragic hero gave rein to his enthusiasm, we plunged ahead with him; we did not think—we surely were not meant to think: "Yes, she is fair; not quite so fair; but fair." The classical function of tragedy would not have been served if we had kept thus aloof. Nor when we treat them as pure poetry, rather than as the clothing for a dramatic action, do the lines support, but on the contrary, they contradict, the definitions of hyperbole quoted above; for the tenor in every case is "thou"—a cipher, a pronoun, a blank upon which no reflexive judgment whatever can be made.

Professor Gans has elsewhere illustrated the point of his definition with the following example: If I say that I went to a party last night, and that there were *millions of people* there, my hyperbole is not meant to be taken as literal truth, but as a sign that there were very many people at the party. Yes; but we should still object that this is not a literary example. The speaker has not employed an artifice in order to move or deceive the listener. When Marlowe's Orcanes, on the other hand, predicts to the "egregious viceroys," that

> Though from the shortest northern parallel,
> Vast Greenland, compass'd with the frozen Sea,
> *Millions of soldiers* cut the Arctic line,
> Bringing the strength of Europe to these arms,
> Our Turkey blades shall glide through all their throats,[24]

we do not pause to reflect that he is probably exaggerating. Rather, if the hyperbole has worked, "we are filled with a proud exaltation and a sense of vaunting joy, as though we had ourselves produced what we had heard."[25] We do not collect our wits and subdue our feelings in order to determine the exact portion of truth in what he says, but strive to overtop him on his own high ground, declaring, with a hubris even more superb than his, that one hundred myriads is too small a number to describe the multitude that fills our mind.

Textual analysis is not, however, the only basis for our claim that contemporary critics have misunderstood the nature of hyperbole. There is also an historical reason[26] to believe so. If there were not, we should, as we said, almost certainly have discarded a conclusion which makes of hyperbole a unique exception to the rule of literariness—the rule according to which a text is literary if it "does not mean what it says and means what it does not say."[27] For we have concluded nothing less than that. By showing that enthusiasm is essential to the success of hyperbole, we have shown that hyperbole is meant to be *believed.* When Orcanes boasted that "millions of soldiers" would die beneath his sword, he meant what he said; when Professor Gans's party-goer named the same figure, he meant something else; yet the former is a literary, the latter an unliterary use of hyperbole. In Coleridge's "principle of suspended comparison" we think we have found an historical corroboration of our view. Keeping in mind the extent to which the Romantics relied on hyperbole as a means of attaining the sublime, what should we infer from Coleridge's asseveration, that "an object [is] sublime in relation to which the exercise of comparison is suspended"?[28] What *can* we infer from it, but that the triumph of hyperbole is only complete when enthusiasm so prevails with us, that we cannot begin to form a "reflexive judgment" of its accuracy?

If twentieth-century critics have not appreciated the full meaning of hyperbole, it is doubtless because they have clung too tenaciously to their ability to see through it. The political applications of blind enthusiasm have never been more terrible than in the last fifty years; and it should be as much a source of consolation as of regret to observe, that the fires through which the race has passed have somewhat annealed the sensibilities of the survivors. As J. W. M. Turner once remarked, "the sublime and the ridiculous are often so nearly related that it is difficult to class them separately. One step above the sublime becomes ridiculous and one step above the ridiculous makes the sublime again."[29] That we nowadays hesitate to take the first step lest it should lead to the second, is a sign of greater wisdom in us—a sign that we have taught ourselves not to laugh too lightly at the absurd.

Chapter Nine

Postponement of discussion of hyperbole in Mallarmé. Synopsis of Kant's "Analytic of the Sublime." Objections to applying his theory to literature refuted. Literary version of his theory.

We must now impose further on the patience of the reader who, confidently expecting that the omission would soon be repaired, has forborne to complain that nowhere, in the course of a fairly discursive exposition, have we set forth the ideas and opinions of Mallarmé himself on the subject of hyperbole. It will be objected that, unless we meant to devote the very next section of our argument to that end, we should not have let such opportunities for comparison as arose along the way, slip by. When we used the term "second best" to describe the vehicle of Marlovian hyperbole, for example, we might conveniently have paused to consider the implications of Mallarmé's famous riddle: "*La Pénultième/Est morte*."[1] When we found a proof in the effusions of John Dennis and Coleridge that enthusiasm gives rise to the impulse to *name* things, and another proof in the hyperbole of Marlowe that by organizing names in an open-ended structure the poet can make them less objectionable to the reader, we had done all that was necessary (it might be supposed) to justify the step of proceeding immediately to examine Mallarmé's critique of hyperbole, the "Prose (pour des esseintes)." We could then have shown how Mallarmé manages in that poem to "substituer l'intention d'hyperbole à l'hyperbole elle-même, qui ne subsiste qu'ironiquement défigurée"[2]; how, by invoking the figure of hyperbole at the outset, he throws away his chance of producing its effect on our mind; but how, in compensation for this loss, we are fortified against the spell of the narrative, and can follow the irreversible sequence of incidents that comprise it, without mistaking "l'effet relatif du contenu" for "la visée transcendantale de la forme."[3] If, however, we had raised these matters before adding to our store of observations on the nature of the sublime, those of Immanuel Kant, we should not have been able to develop them as fully and satisfactorily as we hope to do. In particular, the resemblance between Mallarmé's procedure of substituting an idea of hyperbole for its rhetorical effect, and Kant's discovery that, in the sublime moment, we substitute an idea of infinity for our imaginative impression of the same, must have gone unnoticed.

The following summary refers not to the "Observations on the Feeling of the Beautiful and the Sublime" of 1764 but to the second book of the *Critique of Aesthetic Judgement*, entitled "Analytic of the Sublime." The former work, which predates the latter by some twenty-five years, offers scant ground to support the widely held view, that "Kant is as important for any theory of the sublime as Aristotle is for the theory of tragedy,"[4] consisting as it does in large part of dubious epigrams and assertions in the manner of Burke, e.g.: "Night is sublime, day is beautiful," "The sublime moves, the beautiful charms," "Understanding is sublime, wit is beautiful," "Sublime attributes stimulate esteem, beautiful ones, love," etc.[5] By applying his general theory of aesthetic judgment to the experience of the sublime, however, Kant produced in the "Analytic" a more convincing account of that experience than any that had gone before.[6]

The peculiar distinction of the sublime in Kant's philosophy is that it bridges the "immeasurable gulf . . . between the sensible realm of the concept of nature and the supersensible realm of the concept of freedom."[7] Since the most basic contention of the *Critique of Aesthetic Judgment* is that the aesthetic experience, no less than the theoretical and the practical, originates in a priori principles which are universally valid and necessary, involving as they do the three fundamental cognitive faculties of understanding, reason and judgment, the sublime appears to possess a crucial importance not only in the body of thought described by the three *Critiques*, but in the entire history of Western aesthetics from ancient times to the present. For Kant's contention that the judgments of beauty and sublimity are grounded in something identical in all men, implies that the basis of such judgments is formal rather than sensational: "a pure judgment of taste has for its determining ground neither charm nor emotion—in a word, no sensation as the material of the aesthetical judgment." If the sublime is truly a universal experience, therefore, it "can only be cognized . . . through a concept."[8] We cannot communicate the sensations involved in an experience of the sublime, but only our knowledge about the structure of that experience: for the sensations are accidental and unrepeatable,[9] while the structure is constant and universal. The "Analytic of the Sublime" thus represents a radical advance on the sensational theories of the sublime discussed in our fifth and seventh chapters.

Kant divides the sublime into two modes: the mathematical, which "concerns the effect of magnitude on the imagination and is referred to the faculty of cognition," and the dynamical, which "concerns the effect of power (*Macht*) and is referred to the faculty of desire."[10] Both modes involve the subject in a mental operation of three stages. In the first stage the mind and the object of its attention are in harmony: no excess or incongruity on either side disrupts the process of representation (*Vorstellung*). The experience of the beautiful (i.e. of "the sensuous appearance of the ideal") takes place at this stage, and involves no departure from it, because the act of comprehension (*Zusammenfassung*) is carried out with complete success. But in the experience of the sublime the mind fails to comprehend its object. A feeling of displeasure (*Unlust*) arises during a second stage of inconclusive grappling with *too much* or *too many*. In stage three, however, "reason intervenes and presents the idea of totality or infinitude"[11] to the mind, which is saved as a whole from the collapse of one of its parts (the imagination). The sublime experience is hence described as "contrafinal" (*zweckwidrig*) for the imagination, but "final" (*zweckmässig*) for "the whole province of the mind" (*die ganze Bestimmung des Gemüths*).[12] The pretention to ideality of the natural world—the world of phenomena—is discredited at this stage: it is seen to have been wrongly allowed "by virtue of a certain 'subreption' whereby we substitute[d] 'a respect (*Achtung*) for the Object in place of one for the idea of humanity in our own self—the Subject.' "[13] Indeed, the very plausibility of this pretention is what now brings about its exposure and defeat; for the mind reacts to the incomprehensible by turning in on itself; and as it "is led to recognize in the idea of the supersensible its ultimate destiny (*Bestimmung*), it experiences 'a simultaneously awakened pleasure,' since it finds 'the absolutely great only in the proper estate of the Subject.' "[14]

But although this proof of our connection, through reason, with the absolutely great, is "a source of the highest satisfaction"[15] to us, it is yet a satisfaction which we, as natural beings, do not comfortably receive. The infinite presents itself to the mind as an abstract idea; as such it eludes the grasp of the sensible imagination. Therefore

> delight in the sublime in nature is only *negative* (whereas that in the beautiful is *positive*): that is to say it is a feeling of imagination by its own act depriving itself of its freedom by receiving a final determination in accordance with a law other than that of its empirical employment. In this way it

> gains an extension and a power greater than that which it sacrifices. But the ground of this is concealed from it, and in its place it *feels* the sacrifice or deprivation, as well as its cause, to which it is subjected.[16]

The sublime "is what pleases immediately by reason of its opposition to the interest of sense"[17]—or, to apply the term more properly to the psychological effects of "what pleases," it is the "peculiar state of mind" produced by the "aggrandizement of reason at the expense of reality and the imaginative apprehension of reality." Since, moreover, in the larger context of Kant's metaphysics, reason's ideas are an assurance of our supersensible destiny (*Bestimmung*), their trump-cardlike function in the sublime moment makes the latter "*apocalyptic*, in the strict sense that it reveals final things: the defeat of the sensible imagination accomplishes subjectively the end of the natural order."[18]

It will not be necessary, for our purpose of relating these ideas to the prose of Mallarmé, to describe the objections which have been levelled against them as philosophical propositions. Whether Kant fails to explain, for example, why the imagination cannot participate in the pleasure which the whole mind takes in the triumph of reason, or whether he was right to suppose the existence a priori of a transcendent order that is the source of our *Bestimmung* (instead of identifying in the latter, as many critics since Freud have done, a sublimation of more primitive desires), are questions which the literary analyst need not attempt to answer before he can discuss the significance of, say, *l'azur* as a symbol of the ideal. But the fact that Kant was concerned exclusively with the natural sublime, and did not apparently intend that his theory should be applied without modification to literature, bears directly on our undertaking. We can, however, at least find in the necessity for disposing of this fact, an opportunity to make good our promise, that we would describe in more detail the points in the scholarly controversy mentioned in chapter one.

That controversy was begun in 1936 by R. S. Crane who charged, in a review of Samuel Monk's *The Sublime: A Study of Critical Theories in XVIII-Century England*, that the author had failed to distinguish between two entirely dissimilar classes of writers: those who meant by the word "sublime" "the 'Sublime' of Longinus, i.e. that quality difficult to define but easily detectable by sensitive minds familiar with great masterpieces, which gives distinction to literature and plastic art," and those who

> sought the "Sublime" not primarily in works of literature or plastic art but in natural objects of one kind or another, and more particularly in the states of mind which such objects have the power to induce in human spectators. Though their vocabulary was borrowed in part from Longinus, their essential preoccupation separated them sharply from that ancient rhetorician and his modern disciples; their characteristic subject-matter was not compositions and authors but "the pleasures of the imagination" . . .; they were psychologists inquiring about the emotions, not critics investigating the sources of high excellence in art.[19]

It is no coincidence that this objection should have seemed especially "penetrating"[20] to a critic who believed it to be accurate, in the first place, as a statement of historical fact. And indeed there would be grounds for asking whether Mr. Crane had not detected a more fundamental difference in the way the human mind reacts to natural, as opposed to artificial stimuli, than the difference to be inferred from his mere observation that the Augustans upheld a rigid standard of literary propriety, if, as his supporter Ernest Tuveson alleged, "the ancients [really] knew nothing . . . of that sentimental love of the beautiful and sublime in nature, which mountains, sea and landscape exercise upon the modern mind."[21] But we have seen that Longinus himself recurred repeatedly to the natural world for his illustrations of rhetorical sublimity; and although we emphasized, as much as anyone, the remoteness of his *hupsous* from the sublime of Johnson and Coleridge, we also noticed that he used phrases like "hurricane onslaught," "descending thunderbolt," "flash of lightning" and "wide-spreading conflagration" to characterize the eloquence of Demosthenes and Cicero; and that he compared the possessors of great rhetorical gifts to "the craters of Etna, vomiting forth whole mountains [and] rivers of pure Titanian fire."[22] Does it alter the quality of these images, or detract from the sense of violent extension through space which they convey, to observe that they refer, in Longinus's treatise, to the work of the artist, and in the poetry of Thomson and Young, to that of nature? The denotation in both cases is at a remove from reality.

Doubt was first cast on the justice of Crane's strictures, however, not by a theorist, but by an historian of literature. Marjorie Nicolson began the assimilation of the natural to the rhetorical sublime when she pointed out, that the Longinian critics of the eighteenth century "offered some assistance in vocabulary"[23] to the members of a school whose enthusiasm for thunderbolts and hurricanes had been conceived before the vogue of *Peri Hupsous* in England. That assistance could not have been offered if the "quality which gives distinction to literature" had not tended to manifest itself in images of the same kind as those which Crane's psychologists enjoyed. Such has been the opinion of most recent contributors to the dispute. "Greatness in poetry . . . duplicates the pleasurable effects of greatness in nature . . . by 'striking the imagination' as smartly as external objects do," according to W. P. Albrecht.[24] In Paul Goodman's definition of the sublime as "actual experience of a tendency of combinations to break the aesthetic surface,"[25] the last two nouns seem to have been chosen for their inclusiveness. Most explicitly of all, Thomas Weiskel has declared: "For Kant's *Gegenstand der natur* (object of nature) we may substitute *any* object (a line of poetry, for example), which leads us to a formulation something like this: We call an object sublime if the attempt to represent it determines the mind to regard its inability to grasp wholly the object as a symbol of the mind's relation to a transcendent order."[26]

Once the propriety of this identification has been conceded, an enormous advantage devolves from the enthusiast for nature to the student of literature. Mr. Weiskel has already shown that the two sorts of overload mentioned in the "Analytic"—the mathematical and dynamical—correspond to breakdowns in the two operational axes of language described by Roman Jakobson,[27] in such a way that the literary equivalent of Kant's numerical excess produces a temporary "contiguity disorder" in the reader—a failure to sustain the writer's pace of metonymic progression—while too much metaphorical significance (the equivalent of Kant's excess of power) will give him a touch of "similarity disorder." Since the natural and rhetorical sublimes are "structurally cognate,"[28] Weiskel argues, we may substitute for the terms "mind" and "object" which Kant employs to write about the former, the terms "signified" and "signifier" in our investigation of the latter. Just as the untroubled communion of mind and object was disrupted, in the second stage of the mathematical sublime, by a sudden multiplication of the objects of attention beyond the mind's capacity to absorb, so in the act of reading we may find ourselves driven from the position of vantage which we occupied with a feeble tenure in fact, yet with a complacency not very surprising in the party holding the book, and prepared at any moment to shut it, by a sudden copious volley of signifiers striking upon our consciousness. But if, on the other hand, we should be "caught up in a word (or any signifying segment) which seems to 'contain' so much that there is nothing we cannot 'read into' it,"[29] then we shall know sensations not unlike those to which the second stage of Kant's dynamical sublime give rise. The two types of aphasia are resolved as one might expect. In order to transcend the unpleasant second stage of the mathematical sublime, the reader must discover in his own mind a signified great enough to accommodate the surplus of signifiers that vexes his imagination. This he does by regarding "the residue of signifier (in the object) which finds no reflected signified in his own mind—that very indeterminacy—as symbolizing the mind's relation to a transcendent order." Thus

> the absence of a signified itself assumes the status of a signifier, disposing us to feel that behind this newly significant absence lurks a newly discovered presence. . . . (*Unerreichbarkeit*) is regarded as a "presentation" (*Darstellung*): indeterminacy signfies.[30]

The third stage of the mathematical sublime, then, is attained by inserting a substituted term, a metaphor, into the syntagma, so as to reduce its excessive diachronic momentum. In the dynamical sublime the process is reversed. There we must recover the temporal dimension of a text, and escape from the "word or signifying segment" into which our mind has fallen as into Wordsworth's "abyss of idealism."[31] This can only be done by "displacing the excess of signified into the dimension of contiguity," an undertaking which characteristically involves the use of "elision, in response to the danger of stasis or fixation."[32]

Thus recast in the language of Jakobson and Saussure, Kant's ideas are fit to be applied to the writings of Mallarmé. The application will prove more interesting, however, if we do not use the ideas straight, but rather in conjunction with our own. Therefore the next step is to show how the mathematical and dynamical sublimes, in their literary guises, relate to the principles of irony and enthusiasm, and to the figure of hyperbole, as we described them in chapters seven and eight.

Chapter Ten

Phases of Kant's sublime moment related to positions on scale of height and depth. Inferior position assigned by enthusiasm (Burke). *Bathos* the literary result of unqualified enthusiasm. Argument of Kant's "Analytic" disputed by enthusiasts. Subliminal influence of irony on enthusiasts. Methods of completing Kant's sublime moment by introducing irony without subject's conscious knowledge. A new criterion of the sublime.

Whether the sublime is considered in its natural or rhetorical aspect, it implies a relationship of the conscious subject to the abyss. The transition from an inferior to a superior position on the scale of height and depth—from a sense of horror and oppression and personal insignificance to one of godlike exaltation—is precisely the transition which Kant described in the second and third phases of the sublime moment. A new hypothesis may now be proposed: that the writers who trusted most in the power of enthusiasm to give the names for things the quality of the things themselves, are the same writers who failed to progress beyond Kant's second phase, and who dwelt, in consequence, largely or exclusively on the element of horror in the sublime.

The repudiation of reason is nowhere more strenuous or

thorough-going than in Burke's *Inquiry*, where the varieties of natural and literary sublimity are given a categorical arrangement. Let it be said at once, that Burke's table of contents features not a single entry to which Kant, or for that matter any late-eighteenth-century amateur of the sublime would have objected; but that, in every case, the effectiveness of the entry as a means of bringing about the whole experience of the sublime depends on its effectiveness in thwarting or suspending the operation of reason—on its capacity, that is, to forestall the transition to Kant's third stage. Passages such as that in which he extolls the emotion of fear (which more than any other "effectually robs the mind of all its powers of acting and reasoning," and is therefore, like astonishment, "an effect of the sublime in its highest degree")[1] are the same passages which, on the one hand, have brought down on Burke's reputation the censure of metaphysicians from Coleridge to A. C. Bradley,[2] and which, on the other, must be cited to account for the popularity of his treatise in his own age. In our fifth chapter we noticed that the writers who advertised their relish for fearsome natural spectacles held in common a pair of complementary beliefs: first, that the sort of aesthetic erethism (so to call it) which delights in representations of suffering and terror, may be cultivated without moral blame, provided that an idea of the glory of God can also be derived from them; and second, that in a world so powerfully charged with the authority of God, and charged, in proportion, with meaning for the faithful, the poet *should* expect the signifier "avalanche" to produce as vivid a signified in the reader's mind as any avalanche-referent would do.[3] (The second of these beliefs accounts, for instance, for James Thomson's practice of revising his long descriptive poem *The Seasons* [1726-1730, 1746,] not with the purpose of adjusting his verses to the actual cast of his mind, but to ensure that they contained no expressions at variance with the latest "scientific information and theories.")[4] From these several facts we may conclude, that religious faith, alias "enthusiasm sealed off from doubt," has a twofold effect on the conscious subject, enabling him to discover sublimity in prospects and sensations of a kind that strike the skeptical mind as merely horrible; and to discover it also in writing which the same mind thinks naive. On the scale of height and depth, naive writing leads to the opposite of *hupsous* (elevation); it leads to *bathos* (the profound).

That the word "bathos" should be more widely understood in the sense given it by Pope in 1727, of "a ludicrous descent from the elevated to the commonplace," than in its stricter, earlier, unsatirical sense,[5] is all to the good of the present argument. It is a fact which bespeaks a want of enthusiasm in Pope, who used the word for the first time in a virulent parody of *Peri Hupsous*; and in the generality of readers, who receive it in ignorance of its simpler meaning. "Bathos" has been so much on the lips of the ironist, however, that, like the words "artificial," "sentimental," "condescending," and "worthy," it will appear to everyone but the pedant who employs it literally, to mean the opposite of what he intends. For "bathos," then, let us substitute the description of a tendency and an attitude: the tendency to overlook the difference between language and reality; and the attitude that allowed Coleridge to enjoy the belief (momentarily excited by his passage through the cathedral at Rheims) that "I am nothing"[6]; the same "attitude of inward prostration"[7] recommended by William Gladstone to himself, and of Samuel Johnson in the Buller of Buchan, where "a natural wall, rising steep on every side to a [tremendous] height, produced [an idea sublime in the extreme,] the idea of insurmountable confinement."[8] The importance of faith for the holding of this attitude was sufficiently belabored in an earlier chapter; we may recall it now, however, in connection with the Kantian doctrine of "subreption." That is the delusive movement of mind in which the subject mistakes the real for the ideal, the natural for the absolute. Subreption occurs in the second stage of Kant's sublime moment and is corrected in the third. Yet a whole class of writers has been content not to expose the cheat of subreption; not to rise from the bottom of the scale; not to exchange oppression for serenity; not to sweeten terror with reflection. This class is much larger than the school of Burke, which it notably includes; it is comprised of all writers in whom the impulse to wallow in reality predominates over the impulse to despise it. And since writers of this description have tended to press their claim to the mantle of Longinus more urgently than the ironists have done; since they have memorably, if arbitrarily, affixed the device of sublimity to the banner of their cause, we find ourselves confronted with a basic choice of explanations: either Kant was wrong, and no transition to a third stage of spiritual self-congratulation is necessary for the attainment of the sublime; or the enthusiasts, the devout sensationalists, the believers in the divinity of the world, the multitude of unreflecting namers for whom, as for Thomas Gray, "not a precipice, not a torrent, not a cliff [one might encounter,] but is pregnant with religion and poetry,"[9]—the advocates, in short, of the natural sublime, were in fact less unself-conscious than they made themselves out to be, or than they told themselves they were.

The defender of the first explanation, remembering that the burden of proof rests with the affirmative, has only to discredit his opponent's assertion, that the image of an "axis of height and depth" springs to mind from something in the nature of the sublime experience itself, and is not an irrelevant fabrication. This he might try to do by invoking the authority of D. A. Russell, who notes that the Greek words for "height" and "size" (*hupsous* and *megethos*) "are in fact synonyms"[10] in Longinus's treatise; and by adding that in Latin, the language from which the English word "sublime" derives, there is only one word, *altitudo*, to cover the senses of height and depth. But although these facts suggest that the ancients may not have conceived of the sublime moment as of a sudden leap from below to above, they still do not counter the thrust of the second explanation, which is, that the subject *must* feel his superiority to the daunting natural or artificial object at hand (a superiority conferred by his ability to reason) whether he is aware that he feels it or not.[11] Kant's second and third stages may be telescoped, but the third stage may not be eliminated altogether. Now if this explanation is correct, it should be possible to discover in the most enthusiastic text which is also truly sublime, the rhetorical means by which the reader's sense of his superiority to the things described is *subliminally* conveyed to him.

That hyperbole is not such a means, no persuaded reader of our seventh and eighth chapters will deny. Reflection is impossible when hyperbole is in force, for by commanding our enthusiasm, hyperbole induces us to believe what we are told. Hyperbole might even be defined as the rhetorical equivalent of subreption. It disposes the mind to move on to the third stage and consummation of the sublime experience. One obvious method of effecting this transition is to divide the subject into two *dramatis personae*, the second of whom comments with astonished sobriety on the hyperbolic vehemence of the first. In the climax of the challenge scene of *Richard II*, for example, the sublime thrill is not imparted until *after* the king has pronounced, *sotto voce*, on the mettle of the foaming Bolingbroke:

> *Bolingbroke:*
> Further I say, and further will maintain
> Upon his bad life to make all this good,
> That he did plot the Duke of Gloucester's death,
> Suggest his soon-believing adversaries,
> And consequently, like a traitor coward,
> Sluiced out his innocent soul through streams of blood;
> Which blood, like sacrificing Abel's, cries
> *Even from the tongueless caverns of the earth*
> To me, for justice and rough chastisement.
> And by the glorious worth of my descent,
> This arm shall do it, or this life be spent!
>
> *Richard:*
> (*How high a pitch his resolution soars!*)
>
> (I, i)

(Italics added to point up the coincidence of the imagery of height and depth with the contrasting attitudes of the subject in the second and third stages of the sublime moment.)[12]

The reader's acceptance of what we take to be another method of combining, in a single stage, a sensational awareness of our physical frailty with an esteem for ourselves as beings capable of abstract reasoning, is so important a condition for his approval of the choice of texts to be discussed, in part two, as essays by Mallarmé in the art of the sublime, that we had better preface our description of it by acknowledging, that there are two apparent weaknesses in our position. These are, first, that it is presumptuous to impute to a whole class of writers numbering, after all, many famous names in its ranks, a lack of awareness of the factors that went into the formation of their own aesthetic judgments, while having easy recourse to a term as unsatisfactory, because as insusceptible of clear definition, as the term "subliminal"; and second, that no sooner shall we have allowed the efficiency of this other method as a means of combining the final two stages of the sublime moment in one, than we shall be led, by implication, far away from the familiar décor and restricted apparatus of late-eighteenth-century sublimity, which some readers may still consider essential for the production of the sublime experience, properly so called.

We cannot refute the first of these objections more decisively than by examining a pair of Coleridge's remarks. He alleges that Kant erred in defining the sublime object as one "in comparison with which everything else appears small," since according to Coleridge, the "sublime object admits of no comparison."[13] This criticism is valuable as a profession of faith by Coleridge, who allies himself by means of it with the writers of every age who have maintained that reason has no place in the experience of sublimity; but it has no value as a detection of error in Kant, answering as it does to an interpretation by Herder, rather than to the original.[14] He then observes, that

> The sun-smitten mountain is beautiful, in virtue of what it actually and directly presents to the senses; the cloud-capped mountain is sublime, in virtue of the idea of infinity which it suggests to the mind.

The wording of this distinction gives color to our argument. For Coleridge *knows* that the cloud-capped mountain is not infinite: it merely "presents to the senses" an appearance which gives rise to the notion of infinity. It is therefore sublime because it causes him to conceive of infinity as something other than what he rationally knows the mountain to be. In the word "suggests" lurks the act of comparison; but Coleridge will not countenance this act, preferring instead to believe that his mind is completely "chained to the object."[15] It is a preference dictated by enthusiasm, which would require him to take the view that the mind is a mere sensorium. This view he did not take; and it is logical to assume that, in the present case, his powers of comparison are being exercised below the threshold of his awareness.

The second objection is best answered by a consideration of actual examples. We shall examine two texts that afford the reader a sense of his connection with the absolute, without requiring him to undergo an ordeal such as the eighteenth-century model required. These texts engage the subject's capacity to admire a representation of impressive natural objects *and* his capacity to conceive an abstraction greater than those objects. In both texts the structure of the sublime experience is fulfilled; yet from both the machinery of terror is missing.

This other method of provoking the subject to reflect on his superiority to the object, without allowing him to realize that he has ceased to regard the object as unsurpassably great, is to introduce a human scale of measurement into the representation—a human figure into the landscape, or a human motive into the natural history. In this way, the key to the undoing of the subreption is contained in the representation of the object itself. The subject is not made aware of a difference between himself and the object, but of a tension between two elements in the representation. His need to assert his own peculiar excellence in the face of the object is gratified when he perceives that a symbol of humanity has been included in the representation. Hence he is not thrown back upon himself (so far as he is aware) but continues to admire the object, i.e. the loaded representation.

This method has been so often and successfully practiced with the avowed aim of rendering one's efforts sublime, that the circumstance of its having been overlooked, until now, by every examiner of that quality, would appear very remarkable, if we did not recall that the stock of personification as a literary trope has fallen constantly since the eighteenth century; and that the orthodoxy of modern taste instructs us to deplore the Pathetic Fallacy.[16] The circumstance might be construed as another proof that this method only works when the human element is not blatantly introduced into the representation. We accept, for example, Sir Walter Scott's assurance that the Highland cataract which he describes in chapter thirty-five of *Rob Roy*, is "well calculated to impress strangers with some feelings of awe," because we respond without the interference of our intellect to the tension between the series of anthropopathic verbs in the description—"hurling its waters . . . leaps . . . precipitous dash . . . hurried . . . escaped . . ."—and the plain fact, also given, that the fall is "at least fifty feet in depth." Likewise, but on an even greater scale, we can trace our exhilaration before the picture of *Belshazzar's Feast* by John Martin (a work, according to Charles Lamb, of "the highest order of the material sublime,")[17] to our perception at one and the same moment, of the diminutive figures in the foreground and the architectural vista behind.[18] In both cases, the symbolic inclusion of the subject in the representation has the effect of bringing home to him a sense of his smallness and vulnerability relative to the object; but this sense of disproportion is as satisfying as it is frightening to him, since it bears manifestly only on the symbol, the objectification, of the subject, not on the subject himself. He therefore feels neither directly threatened nor absolutely safe. He is not scared out of his wits; neither is he indifferent to the fate of his representative. Enthusiasm does not blind him to his otherness; but irony does not attune him to that alone. He is simultaneously *below* and *above* the world of phenomena, participating in it through his senses, yet transcending it with his mind.

The final implication of this method will unfold after a reading of two more passages, the first from William Cowper's *The Task* (1785), the second from Joseph Conrad's short story "Youth" (1898):

> Come evening once again, season of peace,
> Return sweet evening, and continue long!
> Methinks I see thee in the streaky west,
> With matron-step slow-moving, while the night
> Treads on thy sweeping train; one hand employ'd
> In letting fall the curtain of repose
> On bird and beast, the other charged for man
> With sweet oblivion of the cares of day;
> Not sumptuously adorn'd, nor needing aid
> Like homely featur'd night, of clust'ring gems,
> A star or two just twinkling on thy brow
> Suffices thee; save that the moon is thine
> No less than hers, not worn indeed on high
> With ostentatious pageantry, but set
> With modest grandeur in thy purple zone,
> Resplendent less, but of an ampler round.
> (Book IV, lines 243–258)

> And this is how I see the East. I have seen its secret places and have looked into its very soul; but now I see it always from a small boat, a high outline of mountains, blue and afar in the morning; like faint mist at noon; a jagged wall of purple at sunset. I have the feel of the oar in my hand, the vision of a scorching blue sea in my eyes. And I see a bay, a

> wide bay, smooth as glass and polished like ice, shimmering in the dark. A red light burns far off upon the gloom of the land, and the night is soft and warm. We drag at the oars with aching arms, and suddenly a puff of wind, a puff faint and tepid and laden with strange odours of blossoms, of aromatic wood, comes out of the still night—the first sigh of the East on my face. That I can never forget. It was impalpable and enslaving, like a charm, like a whispered promise of mysterious delight.

Both these passages conform to the requirement for sublimity proposed above, in that they both begin by setting up two oppositely charged poles of interest in the reader's mind—the human and the natural; proceed to concentrate on one of the poles at the expense of the other; and conclude by reminding us suddenly of the pole whose claims have been neglected in the course of the description. At that moment a sort of discharge takes place: the reader feels the claims of the subject and the object simultaneously; and at once aloof and involved, he undergoes Kant's expansion of soul *without* withdrawing his attention from the representation or consciously reflecting on himself. The two passages are companion pieces in this respect, that although the point of discharge (which may be located in the phrases "save that the moon is thine" and "the first sigh of the East on my face") is reached by a different route in each of them—Cowper developing mainly the human code up to that point, and Conrad mainly the natural—yet it is reached in both cases within the genre of the nocturne, and without the use of hurricanes, thunderbolts or other violent paraphernalia.

An adequate criterion of the sublime, then, must not stipulate that the subject should be overwrought or terrified in the second stage. It must be cast instead in terms that can accommodate *any* object having the power to give him a sense of the disproportion between his status as a creature of ideas, and the status of the material world in which he lives. If the subject's attitude is more enthusiastic than ironic, we may expect the furniture of the second stage to be highly prepossessing, and of the sort familiar to readers of the Gothic romance. But when irony has the edge, the object dwindles in importance; the third stage largely subsumes the second, and the experience is not terrific but serene. Yet the subject cannot be devoid of enthusiasm any more than of irony, for without both qualities no expansion of soul will take place; no discharge of emotion between the two loci of his consciousness: *below* and *above* the object of representation, or *before* and *after* being taken in by it.

The sublime that arises from a humble occasion will never usurp the place of its roaring counterpart in the public mind, if for no other reason than that there has been so much work in the latter vein, attracting notice at first by its stridency, and remaining to clog the bibliographies of scholars; while a tradition of the serene sublime must be eked out with remarks such as Coleridge's that "Shakespeare drops a handkerchief, and [sublime] effects follow,"[19] or A. C. Bradley's, that "Wordsworth's six-year-old child and Turgenief's sparrow"[20] are sublime; with a reference to Ann Radcliffe's idea that the sublime can occur in moderation,[21] or to a phrase in *Melmoth the Wanderer*, "sublime and yet softened"[22]; with a comparison of the sublimity of distant mountains in *Waverley*,[23] to that which the eighteenth-century traveller only experienced when he had penetrated deep into the Alps[24]; and with the few texts, such as Ruskin's famous description of Europe from a bird's-eye view,[25] in which the superior position is attained after a minimum of time-serving in the second stage. By establishing that the sublime can occur in an intimate or domestic context, however, we have removed the last of the theoretical impediments in the way to our goal, which has always been to vindicate the relevance of the notion of the sublime to a close reading of Mallarmé's prose.

Chapter Eleven

Mallarmé eligible for consideration as a practitioner of the sublime by both old and new standards. His obscurity the product of irony; contrasted to obscurity of enthusiasts. His experiment in sublimation. A paradox: the theoretical impossibility of his practice of the sublime. Literary result of the paradox: a singular treatment of hyperbole.

There were, of course, prima facie grounds for the adoption of our proposal. Mallarmé's preoccupation with the theme of the abyss, for example, is apparent in such works as *Igitur*, his "intellectual drama" of the myth of Icarus; in "Les Fenêtres" and "L'Azur," where the theme of "insurmountable confinement"[1] is developed; in his wish to explore "l'intime gouffre de chaque pensée"[2]; and in what Jean-Pierre Richard calls his attempts to "se déliverer de la hauteur par un engagement total dans l'abîme."[3] It is also apparent in his love of "choses fanées,"[4] which presented to his mind a perspective on the temporal abyss very similar to that which ruins and relics presented to the Romantics. Then, in his wish to discover "l' architecture une, qui se retrouve en dépit des échafaudages, impeccable dans ses proportions,"[5] he joins the heterogeneous company of Horace Walpole and Sir Donald Tovey, whose respective appreciations of the "sublime"[6] *Carceri* of Piranesi, and of "that greatness of design . . . which is unfailingly sublime, whatever the ostensible range of the subject,"[7] his own metaphor recalls.[8]

If these grounds were not sufficiently convincing in themselves to place the legitimacy of our comparative topic beyond question at the outset, they have since been reinforced by others bearing an even more tangible relation to the sequel. These are the literary implications of our definition of the sublime. The subject can obtain an idea of his disproportion to the object either by inflating the object with enthusiasm at the expense of his own identity or by directing the better part of that enthusiasm along "le chemin mystérieux [qui] va vers l' intérieur"[9]—towards a recognition of his ultimate superiority to any object. He may choose to subordinate his art to the world (to God or politics or any principle that relates adventitiously to aesthetic form) or he may decide, with Mallarmé, that "tout, au monde, existe pour aboutir à un Livre."[10] In the latter case we must not be surprised if slight objects are made the occasion for sublime poetry.[11] We must reflect, instead, on the truth of Coleridge's remark, that

> In *Paradise Lost* the sublimest parts are the revelations of Milton's own mind, producing itself and evolving its own greatness; . . . . so that when that which is merely entertaining for its objective beauty is introduced, it at first seems a discord.[12]

This being so, there is no reason why the structure of the sublime experience should not employ as its objective materials the candied fruits and Easter eggs of Mallarmé's *vers de circonstance.* Such objects are no less real than avalanches; consequently they are no less qualified to provide the occasion for the subject's exercise of his powers of irony and enthusiasm. The sublime, as Longinus was the first to observe, is a matter of treatment. The particular form of the sublime experience that requires prepossessing objects is not the only form; it is simply the form in which enthusiasm preponderates over irony.

The adversary principles of light and dark have always been associated with both the natural and rhetorical sublimes; but the association takes a puzzling form in Mallarmé. His norotious obscurity seems to be the paradoxical result of "l'étreinte ferme et la mise en lumière des mots."[13] It is as though, in his attempt to "instituer une relation entre les images exacte, [pour] que s'en détache un tiers aspect fusible et clair,"[14] he had contrived to remove all the areas of shadow from his poems, in the sense that none of the terms of which they are composed is allowed to retain its mere commercial value, the significance, easily graspable, and as easily relinquishable, which it brings to everyday speech. Such a concession to the clarity of *reportage* would have abated the brilliancy of the "allumage de reflets réciproques comme une virtuelle traînée de feux sur des pierreries" after which he strove.[15] An instructive contrast to the obscurity of Burke and the naive enthusiasts in general may be drawn. Obscurity is illustrated in part two, section three of the *Inquiry* by an excerpt from *Paradise Lost* in which several elements are *said* to be "dim" and "obscur'd." The reader perceives with perfect clarity that dark objects are represented. Still, there is no reason to suppose that the end of obscurity (which is to terrify the subject by impressing him with his ignorance) will not be accomplished in this straightforward manner, provided that the subject is a reader of the sort required by Burke—one, namely, whose enthusiastic engagement with the object of representation may be taken for granted. There is no distinction in observing that, although the object is dark, the subject's mind is clear, unless the subject is aware of a difference between himself and the object. Mallarmé was, however, aware of this difference; he exulted in it, and refused to tender words as things—"sur quoi les pages se refermeraient mal."[16] In his case the obscurity arises in the mind of the reader like a shadow cast by the incandescence of the poem. The thickness of the obscurity is a measure of the reader's comparative failure to duplicate the poet's experiment in sublimation—a term which is intended here to carry its sense as a *mot outil* of physics, denoting the passage of a substance directly from the solid to the gaseous state. The metaphor from physics is an apt reminder, first, that the sublime, in Julia Kristeva's words, "n'a pas d'objet";[17] and second, that the inert component in language cannot be "abolished" "sans traîner les gazes d'origine."[18] For until he learns to convert, by a mental process akin to this physical one, the bulky verbal lumber with which his unliterary ideology of language has saddled him, into "les subdivisions prismatiques de l'Idée," the reader will not be able to "presque refaire" the poem, as Mallarmé invites him to do.[19] Unlike the audience of Longinus's sublime orator, who needed only enthusiasm to feel a "vaunting joy, as though [they themselves] had produced what [they] had heard,"[20] Mallarmé's reader must acquire this special accomplishment before he can taste the "joie délicieuse de croire qu'il crée"[21]—before obscurity will give way to enlightenment in his mind.

To decide the matter of light and dark in Mallarmé thus, however, is to imply that, had he been a more efficient transmitter of his "native illumination,"[22] he would have expunged the thematic presence of obscurity from his poems altogether. But too many and too deliberate are the references to veils and shrouds for it to be supposed that this was his intention; too plainly commendatory the phrases "nuage précieux" and "très subtil nuage," with which he evoked the characters of lace and music.[23] The poet himself seems to have authorized the view, that a "studied ambiguity . . . clings like a haze"[24] to his work. What, then, is the difference between his valuation of obscurity and that of Longinus or Burke?

The answer will lead us directly to the central contradiction in Mallarmé's philosophy of art—a contradiction, already touched upon in chapter six, which may serve as an appropriate envoi to the whole of part one.

For the artist who responds enthusiastically to the natural world, and finds enough of the ideal to suit him in an imposing object, obscurity, like the clouds on Coleridge's mountain, is mere frosting on the cake. Without it, the pleasure afforded by the object is less sweet, perhaps, but scarcely less substantial. But the "Gloire du long désir, Idées"[25] around which Mallarmé builds his poems is not a part of the natural world at all. It is "le Rien qui est la vérite."[26] In thinking of it as *éclat* or *lumière*, we must remember that we are employing a physical metaphor for an immaterial quality. We cannot perceive this *éclat* in itself, but only when it is refracted through words signifying *something*. The more ingeniously the words are arranged, the more completely they will cancel out each other's significance; the closer the poem as a whole will come to signifying nothing, and the more vivid, the less impaired, will be the intimation of the ideal which it affords.[27] Yet a degree of obscurity in the poem, relative to the ideal, the absence, the perspicuous *éclat* which it surrounds, is necessary. Mallarmé's is a *necessary* obscurity, unlike Burke's or Coleridge's; but one which, unlike theirs, coincides only incidentally (not necessarily) with *images* of darkness, clouds, etc. These words happen to be metaphors for the constitutive principle of his poetic technique, just as light was a metaphor for his subject, the ideal. But the principle must not be confused with the theme of obscurity. Having taken such pains to establish, in chapter nine, that the natural and rhetorical sublimes are "structurally cognate,"[28] we must now understand also that "l'originalité de Mallarmé n'est pas dans sa thématique, laquelle n'est jamais qu'une figuration allégorique d'un drame situé dans l'esprit lui-même."[29]

That Mallarmé should labor to clarify a screen of words which the interest of his profession demands he should not allow to become perfectly clear, is only one aspect of the central contradiction mentioned above. Virtually every paradox in his writings can be referred to the following philosophical dilemma, which is posed, in the mind of the observer at least, by the outcome of his famous *ascèse* at Tournon (1866 to 1869):

1. In the course of an "année effrayante," Mallarmé becomes "impersonnel . . . une aptitude qu'a l'Univers Spirituel à se voir et à se développer, à travers ce qui fut moi."[30]

1a. The universe has no ultimate meaning, for God is a "vieux et méchant plumage."[31]

2. Mallarmé avers "que ne vaille de raison pour se considérer Dieu,"[32] yet trusts in his native illumination to order the poetic work.

2a. This native illumination, the "astre en fête"[33] of the poet, is neither the *scintilla animae* of old religion, nor a particle of Hegel's Absolute Spirit. It offers an assurance of the possibility of perfection no more reliable than that of the "plumage."

3. To be true to his own belief, therefore, Mallarmé must not affirm the existence, but only the nonexistence, of the ideal. He keeps faith with himself by qualifying his celebrations of the ideal as fictions and "glorieux mensonges,"[34] and by resorting to the figure of praeteritio when the logic of discourse constrains him to mention it outright. But he fails to keep faith when he refers to the "instinct de ciel en chacun" as though he did not think it a delusion[35]; and when he dismisses René Ghil for refusing to agree that "l'on ne peut se passer d' Eden."[36] He fails, when he ignores the two inescapable corollaries of his disbelief in a source of perfection within or without the poet, which are, that his notion of "l'Indicible ou le Pur, la poésie sans les mots"[37] *must* be a fantasy; and that there can be no such thing as a "sonnet nul et se réfléchissant de toutes les façons," a "Sonnet allégorique de lui-même."[38] He fails, when he entertains, as though it seemed to him a project that might some day be achieved, the project of drafting "un livre architectural et prémédité" which would not be "un recueil des inspirations de hasard."[39] For it is the lesson of *Un Coup de dés*, his latest attempt to transpose "la

pensée pure," that the most considered verbal arrangement is no more necessary than the least, necessity being an absolute condition.[40] Whether or not Mallarmé was satisfied that in every word he had chosen "l'exclusif et le bon,"[41] he still took the precaution to insure against the possible charge of fraud, or at least, of misrepresentation, by including the entire poem inside a statement to the effect, that contingency cannot be eliminated. His "concept originel" is not Being, but its opposite, "le rien de mystère"[42]; therefore he must not expect that he can ever set his work beyond the pale of Becoming. If the *Grand Oeuvre* is to be a "palais,"[43] it will be a palace to which new wings and extensions can be added indefinitely. And if the Book should ever be completed, it will turn out to resemble lesser books; it will be another "coffret spirituel,"[44] of which we may say, that like "the secret casket of his genius, [it] contains a vapour rather than a jewel."[45]

It is not our intention to imply that the beauty of Mallarmé's poetry is diminished by the want of rigor in his philosophy. If we were prepared to venture an editorial opinion at this point in a work primarily analytical and expository, it would merely be that Mallarmé's lapses from the agnosticism prescribed by the strict course of thought he followed at Tournon, into the mysticism of his belief that "le splendide génie éternel n'a pas d' ombre,"[46] and that "le Poète règne sur sa propre idéalité,"[47]—that these lapses appear to us to coincide with the expression of the least attractive aspect of his personality, namely, his considerable self-regard. The narcissism of genius has been observed before now, however[48]; and if we dwell thus particularly on the case of one, to whom it did not occur that he had contradicted himself by declaring that the poet's work consists, from an eternal point of view, of lies, while maintaining that his task should be to "amonceler la clarté radieuse avec des mots qu'il profère comme ceux de *Vérité*,"[49] and who, having proposed himself as the *summum* of negative capability—the "impersonal aptitude" for self-expression of the spiritual universe—should try to "aboli[r] le monde pour faire exister [son] rêve,"[50] we do so only because we anticipate that a sense of Mallarmé's basic philosophical trouble will help us to understand the local contradictions in his poetry.

Chief among these are the figure of oxymoron, a resolved contradiction in terms, of which the phrases "splendeur intime," "gouffre intime" and "type humain absolu"[51] are examples; and the figures of litotes and praeteritio, which indicate a contradiction between real and apparent intentions. It is especially notable that Mallarmé, with his cult of the inward-looking genius and his desire to fashion the self-reflecting work, whould have favored the last two figures, which may be defined as inverted forms of hyperbole. Where Christopher Marlowe's enthusiasm for some object prompted him to exclaim that that object was inherently greater than the greatest specimen of its kind, Mallarmé, who knows in advance that every object will prove to be a dead end, adopts the opposite course. Instead of directing the reader's "puissance d' enthousiasme"[52] *at* something, he directs it *away* from everything. Consequently it is not released from the closed circuit of the poem, but remains with the subject. To state, with Marlowe and the hyperbolists, that one object is more nearly ideal than another because it is more intensely imbued with the property of being an object, is to put in abeyance one's power of conceiving an abstraction greater than any object. It is to fall into the trap of subreption[53] by allowing one's enthusiasm to discharge itself in an affirmation of what Duns Scotus called the *haecceitas*, the "this-ness," of the object.[54] Now Mallarmé knew as well as Kant, that in such an affirmation *foeda est et brevis voluptas.* Enthusiasm should not be expended, but husbanded and withheld, until, in Kant's words, one finds "the absolutely great only in the proper estate of the Subject."[55] Therefore Mallarmé, who believes that the ideal is not what is more than the most but what is less than the least material, must contrive to reverse the normal vector of hyperbole,[56] which points away from the subject. He will not go so far afield as to name even the least substantial object, lest it should tempt the reader to commit his enthusiasm. And he considers that he has accomplished his aim when that enthusiasm, like the kiss of his daughter's fan, "Ne peut jaillir ni s'appaiser."[57] The familiar appointments of his poems comprise an inventory of things not found there: "l'absence . . . de lit" and "l'absente de tous bouquets"; the "aboli bibelot" and the "dentelle [qui] s'abolit"; "nul ptyx," "nul écho," "nul ventre," "nul jour."[58]

It is unthinkable that the objective world should ever run short of invitations for Mallarmé to decline. Another penultimate will always arise behind the one just abolished. In the pleasure he can give us by distinguishing himself from every thing, the poet has a motive for postponing the confrontation from which the philosopher must not shrink: the confrontation with the question of absolute meaning. If it were otherwise, we should have to admit that by detecting what we have called the central flaw in Mallarmé's metaphysics, we had disproved the validity of our own thesis. For the inner ideal to which Kant's subject reverted in the third stage of the sublime moment was the reflection *in parvo* of "a noumenal self-determined Being."[59] Mallarmé, however, refused to postulate such a Being; therefore he could not logically expect that the transition to the third stage would bring about an expansion of soul, rather than a constriction of the same. He could not logically expect it, but he could write poetry as though he did. For if the sound portion of his theory implies the vanity of his practice, the sublime yield of his practice suggests the inconsequence of his theory.[60]

This paradox helps us to explain the dissension among his interpreters. Those who set out, after Jean-Pierre Richard, to draw a "phénoménologie concrète" of the poems, are bound to feel the poet's pleasure in the exercise of his craft, and to find that, like Richard, they have drawn the picture of "un Mallarmé heureux."[61] But those who proceed to the poems from the starting point of the theory, are likely to discuss them as episodes in a career illustrating "le malheur inhérent au génie,"[62] and as incidents of *échec.*

Having diagnosed a paradox, we should be incautious to assert that the whole truth lies in either half of it. The value of the paradox is rather as a model for the organization of part two. We have now to show how the concept of the sublime that appears in Mallarmé's theoretical writings differs from the one just described, and how it differs from what we take to be the sublime quality in some of his prose.

Part Two

Chapter Twelve

The Context of the Word "Sublime" in Mallarmé's Prose.

The word "sublime" appears as an adjective or a substantive ten times in the prose writings of Mallarmé. The first appearance is in the "Symphonie littéraire" of 1864; the last, in the patchwork text of "Crise de vers," published in 1896 but containing material written ten years earlier. The appearance close together in the latter work of phrases containing the word from 1886 and 1895, suggests the consistency of Mallarmé's usage—a consistency which withstood the epistemological trial of his period at Tournon and continued to the end of his life. This consistency is reflected, moreover, in the author's recurrent use of the same rhetorical figures in the context of the word "sublime," whatever the date of composition of the passage in question. We venture, therefore, not to observe in this chapter the obligation to present the ten passages in chronological order—an obligation which might otherwise be expected to prevail in a work of literary scholarship. Instead, we shall take them up in order of ascending interest,[1] and attempt, in the course of our discussion, to unify our conclusions about the separate passages by identifying the themes which they feature in common.

I. *Oeuvres complètes*, pp. 716–719

Three such themes are touched upon, rather than developed at any length, in the "Chronique de Paris" column of the first issue of *La Dernière Mode* (September 1874). These are the themes of the sublime as theatre; of the sublime as a quality that arises independently of attempts to fulfill extra-aesthetic purposes; and of the sublime as the condition under which "virtual" perfection is discovered. The interest of the passage lies not so much in the allusion to the sublime itself as in the context of that allusion; for no sooner has the chronicler stated his view, that "l'art dramatique de notre Temps, vaste, sublime, presque religieux, est à trouver," than he withdraws from the brink of a descent to further grave reflection, and preserves the urbanity of his *ton général* by observing, that "rien ne nous autorise, dans ces causeries prolongées pendant une demi-heure à en formuler l'idéal." In the absence of such a formulation we can gather little of Mallarmé's own notion of the sublime from its highly conventional location, in this passage, between the adjectives "vaste" and "religieux"; for this triple linkage dates back at least to the time of Boileau and Saint-Evremont, if not, indeed, to that of Longinus, and is anything but an original notion here. The association of the sublime with the drama has a pedigree quite as long, the *style sublime* having been considered peculiarly appropriate for the utterances of characters inhabiting the high moral terrain of tragedy.[2] At present we merely note the association against such time as we shall have occasion to consider its recurrence in a more developed text[3] of the author's. (Then, we shall remember that the theatre was presented here as a public forum, where the "lumière réelle du gaz"[4] forbade the concocting of pleasant, private rêveries: the spectators were confronted with the actors on stage, who, in an incompetently contrived work, seemed "les acteurs d'un cauchemar spécial": "Vaines, splendides, incompréhensibles, [ils] proclaim[aient] à haute voix leur sottise.")

The other two themes can be traced, here as elsewhere, to the author's position on the matter of aesthetic utility—a position which he defends without the unbecoming appearance of dogmatism before this fashionable readership. In fact, he does not seem to be altogether serious. Granted the tenability of his familiar view, that what passes for reality is really "Rien, le décor"—a collection of dummies and pasteboard props whose sole self-justification is their capacity to evoke other "sites" and figures somewhat less entrenched in the passing moment than they—and granted, that the "true" lineaments of the ideal have yet to be discovered (or invented, in the original sense of the word), nevertheless, the "triumph" proposed by this chronicler to the artist is not such, probably, as should have tempted the majority of idealists in the class of artists to persevere in their labors. One cannot imagine Milton, for example, agreeing or even affecting to agree, that his primary purpose was to "plaire [aux] femmes," or that he might measure the value of his books by the number of days they were suffered to lie open "comme un flacon, sur les soieries ornées de chimères" of a boudoir. The serious burden of the text is limited to the author's approval of "oeuvres . . . désintéressées, ce qui, pour l'élite, veut dire intéressantes." In that phrase, and in his congratulations to women on their "isolement de la Politique," he declares for the independence of aesthetic purpose and aesthetic experience (including the experience of the sublime) from every other sort of purpose and experience. But when he gives the principle of disinterestedness a local habitation in the persons of his readers, we recognize the note of flattery which he first sounded in the "Placet futile" of 1862. The mere singularity of hearing the praises of disinterestedness sung in the language of flattery (which by definition cannot be disinterested), should not keep us from proceeding to another text, in which the author is not evidently motivated by the desire to earn money.

II. *Oeuvres complètes*, pp. 261-262

In the first section of the "Symphonie littéraire" of 1864, the status of the word "sublime" in Mallarmé's nomenclature is clarified relative to several themes. Although the word is not employed here (as it was later to be) in an unusual sense, its connection with elements in the codes of divinity, humanity, enthusiasm and the ideal should be examined.

The poet portrays himself as a being compact of divine and animal parts. In the first paragraph, after an invocation of the "Muse moderne de l'Impuissance," he declares his intention to commemorate "les jouissances d'une âme purement passive qui n'est que femme encore, et qui demain peut-être sera bête." The word "femme" as it is used here conveys an idea notably different from that of its counterpart in the passage just discussed, the word "dame." The latter sort of woman read poetry in order to "se parer l'âme": she had a practical object in adorning herself: she sought to secure the esteem of her "ami." Her passivity was skin-deep. But the "femme" to whom the poet now likens his soul is a simpler and nobler creature, as may be judged from the intangible return which she expects from her passivity.[5] In both cases, however, though in differing degrees, the soul's latent divinity, its ability to be quickened and raised by the operation of great art, is equated with the feminine principle, as against the base purposefulness of the masculine. Yet the author's attitude to both principles is ambivalent. The word "bête" in this paragraph, and the reference to his "âme trop puissament liée à la Bêtise terrestre" in the next, imply his abhorrence of his lower nature; but, just as plainly, he groups the sovereign attributes of the poet on the side of the masculine principle. These are, above all, his command of the "trésor . . . des Rythmes" (paragraph one), later called "le souvenir du rythme antérieur"[6]; and his learning in the "science mystérieuse du Verbe." But the conscious possession of these attributes makes him ill at ease in the passive role of reader, and he bears with a mixture of resentment and delectation the "aimable supplice" to which the Muse condemns him: "à ne faire que relire . . . les maîtres inaccessibles dont la beauté me désespère."

In view of the importance which we attached, at the end of part one, to the figure of praeteritio as a means of protecting one's enthusiasm from ridicule—a means that permits one to name things while protesting that one is not naming them—we must not fail to notice its informing presence here. Just as the author of the "Chronique de Paris" contrived to place his delighted descriptions of rich stuffs and interiors beyond the reach of the potentially hostile reader by implying that both he and the reader sought a loftier satisfaction than that afforded by "Rien, le décor" (thereby making it impossible for the descriptions to be used as evidence of a reprehensible taste for luxury in the author)—in just this way, Mallarmé would now pass off the six-hundred-odd words, the four paragraphs in which he celebrates his inability to write, by punctuating them with such phrases as "je n'ai plus qu'à me taire" and "je ne saurais même louer ma lecture salvatrice."

In the second and third paragraphs we learn something of the poet's conception of the ideal. For the first time he here suggests, what he was later to advance more pointedly, that the ideal should be distinguished from its setting, and from the artistic means by which a glimpse of it is obtained. (To the setting and the means, rather than to the ideal itself, was he repeatedly to apply the epithet "sublime," as we shall see.) In the third paragraph, the miraculous "adjuvant terrestre"[7] of Gautier's poetry brings about a "transfiguration" in the narrator, such that his "sensation de légèreté se fond peu à peu en une de perfection" and he beholds "la seule lucidité." Yet before learning of this development, we had been given the impression that the narrator was *already* transfigured. The preceding paragraph began with a superlative description of his beatitude:

> C'est une de ces matinées exceptionnelles où mon esprit, miraculeusement lavé des pâles crépuscules de la vie quotidienne, s'éveille dans le Paradis, trop imprégné d'immortalité pour chercher une jouissance, mais regardant autour de soi avec une candeur qui semble n'avoir jamais connu l'exil. Tout ce qui m'environne a désiré revêtir ma pureté; le

> ciel lui-même ne me contredit pas, et son azur . . . a encore perdu l'ironie de sa beauté, qui s'étend au loin adorablement bleu.

Surely (we may be excused for having assumed) there can be nothing better than this. The writer has described a condition beyond desire and beyond the touch of envy. He has described a condition superior even to that of Kant's subject at the conclusion of the sublime experience—for unlike the latter, he has not had to reject his surroundings in order to find the ideal in himself. He has attained the top of the scale of height and depth by eliminating the irony of the sky, not the sky itself—that he embraces. The generous overflow of his contented feelings (which he is at pains to distinguish from enthusiasm) fills in the distance between himself and every object, and relieves him of the obligation to attempt to build a heaven in his thoughts—an obligation which the slightest trace of irony in his attitude might be enough to impose, and which the observant idealist is accustomed to discharging. If irony and exile are usually quite different modes of divorcing the subject from the surroundings into which he was born, they appear to be one and the same in this instance. For from what exile can the narrator have returned to his original home in paradise, if not from an exile into his own captious self—into a cast of mind upon which no object could impinge without seeming to be challenging him to find fault with it?

When, therefore, in paragraph three, the narrator depreciates this beatitude to a mere "sensation de légèreté," he occasions some confusion in the reader—a confusion presently allayed, however, by the reflection that the text as a whole is meant to celebrate the superior exaltation conferred by a perusal of Gautier's poetry. The "état de grâce" of paragraph two merely rendered the narrator fit to be acted upon by the verses of that author—it could not sustain itself—it threatened to decay into "un plus cruel ennui." But having shot off his biggest hyperbolic guns at the preparatory stage, the narrator must now retrench to the comparative platitude of a "sensation de légèreté." Then he can proceed to the following remarkable conclusion, in which the word "sublime" belatedly appears:

> Donc je n'ai plus qu'à me taire, — non que je me plaise dans une extase voisine de la passivité, mais parce que la voix humaine est ici une erreur, comme le lac, sous l'immobile azur que ne tache pas même la blanche lune des matins d'été, se contente de la refléter avec une muette admiration que troublerait brutalement un murmure de ravissement. Toutefois, — au bord de mes yeux calmes s'amasse une larme dont les diamants primitifs n'atteignent pas la noblesse; — est-ce un pleur d'exquise volupté? Ou, peut-être, tout ce qu'il y avait de divin et d'extra-terrestre en moi a-t-il été appelé comme un parfum par cette lecture trop sublime? De quelle source qu'elle naisse, je laisse cette larme, transparente comme mon rêve lucide, raconter qu'à la faveur de cette poésie, née d'elle-même et qui exista dans le répertoire éternel de l'Idéal de tout temps, avant sa moderne émersion du cerveau de l'impeccable artiste, une âme dédaigneuse du banal coup d'aile d'un enthousiasme humain peut atteindre *la plus haute cime de sérénité* où nous ravisse la beauté.

We will argue that this text is constructed entirely under the sign of praeteritio.

First, how extensive through the whole first part of the "Symphonie littéraire" are the roots of the simile introduced by the phrase "comme le lac"? We need not look beyond the passage quoted above to observe, that the narrator claims to resemble the lake as one mute reflector of a superior object resembles another; yet the very phrase that asserts this resemblance, "muette admiration," suggests at the same time the respect in which the narrator is most unlike the lake, and in so doing, prepares us for the incident of the tear. For the narrator might well have written the comparison by way of the word "miroir" instead of "admiration." There was nothing in-the adjective "muette," following upon "me taire,"[8] that required him to select the one of two derivatives from the Latin *mirari* which imputes a will, rather than a mere existence and capacity, to the lake. *Admiration* is a verbal form; *miroir*, a noun. Consequently we are led to look beyond the immediate context of the comparison, and beyond the ostensible equivalency (prolonged in the phrase "*au bord de* mes yeux") of the passive narrator and the passive lake, to discover in the adverb "brutalement" a sign that the narrator—and by contagion the unlake-like lake given to murmuring of its own accord—bears a connection with the beastly sources of creative energy. It is, moreover, a connection which he is reluctant to admit. For "brutalement" pertains to the code begun in the first, and continued in the second paragraph, with the words "bête" and "Bêtise." Yet "brutalement" does not only comport a gesture of deprecation here. By virtue of its position relative to "murmure" in the chiasmus formed by *troublerait brutalement* and *murmure de ravissement*, it also describes *how* the subject mars his perfect replication of the perfect object. No expression of the subject's enthusiasm can be so refined as to fail to mark his difference from the object. The expression of enthusiasm will always denote his separate existence as an unreflecting being. So long as he continues to prefer the perfection, which is not a pleasure, of retaining "the god within," to the pleasure, which is "brutal" in the fairest sense we can give an ugly word, of releasing it in speech or on paper, so long will the difference between the god, the superior object (or "l'azur,") and the mortal, the inferior subject (or "le lac,") not appear to the latter. And so long will no paean to Gautier be raised.

The Baudelairean intertext of "impeccable"[9] at a few lines' distance from the negated verb "tacher" in the description of the sky, indicates one attribute of the ideal in which that element participates jointly with the art of Gautier. But to the defender of our hypothesis concerning the subject's changing position on the axis of height and depth, this attribute of flawlessness is less interesting than another, also indicated: the attribute of supreme loftiness. The same narrator who feared that he could not sustain himself "à la hauteur d'un charme" in which the sky, though appearing "au loin," yet bore no aspect of irony for him, also finds himself uplifted to "*la plus haute cime de sérénité*" by an artist whom he had considered, in the first place, as one of the "maîtres inaccessibles." The "beauté" of the sky no longer seemed ironic from the vantage point of an "hauteur" commensurate with its own. Likewise the "beauté" of the master's art ceased to inspire the subject with despair when, having assumed it inwardly, he accomplished the ascension for the second time.

The catastrophe is described in the shedding of a tear. This tear is the symbolic counterpart of the text, representing, like it, an assertion of the subject's self after his prolonged self-effacement in favor of the object. What are the grounds for this claim? First, the narrator, though he suggests two possible interpretations of the tear's significance without preferring one to the other, does not conceal that in either case, the tear has sprung from him in response to a "lecture *trop* sublime."[10] The tear comports as plainly as the adjective the sense of protest. We can identify the source of this protest quite confidently in the subject's creative "bêtise," thanks to the presence of the verb "naître" here. In order for the birth of the text and the tear to occur, the subject must have indulged his creative impulse. There is no question of his having been absolutely passive. Yet the text is designed to belittle its author's contribution as much as possible. He presents himself as the mother, not the father of his text, Gautier being the ostensible father. And in the metaphor of the tear, he has chosen a somatic excretion which requires of the subject no effort of will to produce, but which, on the contrary, is generally drawn from the subject against his will.[11]

We called the appearance of the word "sublime" in this paragraph "belated" because we thought that, if it had appeared somewhere in the description of the narrator's first beatitude, it would probably not have been accompanied by the intensifying adverb "trop." We should now, however, emphasize the propriety of its conjunction, in this particular text, with the adverb "trop," and the propriety of its occurrence in the final paragraph, lest it should be thought that we intended to ascribe any error or inadvertance to the author. On the contrary, we consider that the phrase "trop sublime" occurs with special propriety in its present situation—at the close of a text, that is to say, which is no less a denunciation of the "banal coup d'aile d'un enthousiasme humain," and of the narrator's own abhorred impulse to create, than it is a panegyric to Gautier, and a celebration of the afflatus reserved for passive vessels. Inasmuch as the text is largely given over to hints and assertions that the narrator would bring about his fall from perfection by speaking any word of his own, the reader is not surprised to find the word "sublime," when it is mentioned at all, mentioned unwillingly, and with the accompaniment of a complaint. If the text had been constructed on the principle of enthusiasm, and couched in the language of hyperbole, then the word "sublime" might have been flung out boldly at an early stage of the narrator's progress. But the text is rather constructed, as we have said, under the sign of praeteritio.

It is an easy matter to expose the presence of that figure here. To the broken vows of silence quoted earlier we may add two more proofs that the narrator fails to carry out his professed intentions. First, if he really feared to desecrate his beatitude by exercising "la voix humaine," why does he admit, why does he not rather conceal that his tear is meant to "raconter" the whole experience? His pretence that his tear is something other than his text, was flimsy enough before he weakened it by selecting a verb so closely bound up with the idea of the human voice. It follows that the decision to weaken it was deliberate; and that the narrator's real intention is not to be silent but to speak. The second proof is even more striking. By concluding his text in the subjunctive mood with the phrase "où nous *ravisse* la beauté," the author gives voice to the very "murmure de *ravissement*" which he had made a show of suppressing not three sentences before. His plan is clear. By assuring us that he knew that any such utterance would derogate its speaker to the level of a brute, he hoped to place himself above the suspicion of being in danger of falling. Once we should have received him as the antagonist of enthusiasm, he might murmur his ravishment undetected. Impervious to the reproach of readers less devious, if not less incontinent, than he—readers who, though they may write of what they read, do not write that they do not write of what they read—he enthusiastically underscores the penultimate phrase of this disingenuous indictment of hyperbole.

One final detail of the text has so far escaped our notice: the phrase "dont les diamants primitifs n'atteignent pas la noblesse."[12] Unfortunately, the text provides no conclusive indication that there is a deliberate play on the verbs *to attaint* and *to attain* here.[13] This is unfortunate because if both verbs had been activated, two readings would have been possible, or rather, one double reading, that would have connected naturally, like the horns of a dilemma, to the body of Mallarmé's metaphysics. Since this double reading would have constituted a highly effective use of praeteritio, it is worth describing, although as matters stand the following paragraph must be taken to refer to a missed opportunity.[14]

To the extent that the narrator regards "la noblesse" with unqualified approval and desire, it is an absolute quality; and to that extent we may treat it as a synonym for "l'Idéal." Now if "atteindre" is allowed to carry only the sense of *to attain*, and if we ignore for a moment the negation that superadds a sense of regret to the verb, then we recognize the attitude suggested by the basic clause as one of enthusiastic aspiration. The narrator *wants* his tears to crystallize into diamonds. He aspires to attain the ideal (in its variant of nobility) by giving it an imperishably real form. His tears, which are already real, must become more so in order to become ideal. This is the very attitude which we diagnosed in John Dennis and the amateurs of the natural sublime; and in the unreasoning sensationalist in Coleridge. It is the attitude that found its most effective expression in the hyperbole of Marlowe. But what if we admit the sense of *to attaint* as well? Then the narrator would appear to be saying, that the latent diamonds in his tears are fortunately not so far gone in the process of becoming hard and real as to offer an insult, by constituting a material contrast, to the ideal. The negation of the verb "atteindre" would denote his relief, as much as his regret. The ideal, he would imply, will remain untainted so long as it is not embodied in a real object, albeit a precious, transparent, self-reflecting and all but indestructible one. He would give himself credit for not having had the presumption to produce a tear or a text so obviously expressive of enthusiasm as to convict him of the crime of sullying the ideal. *That* he should have done, had he persuaded us to forget, that like every ideal quality, "la noblesse" is unattainable. He and we should then have fallen from the sublime height at which we were content to be silent.

Such a play on the verb "atteindre" would have been the subtlest use of praeteritio in a text which in fact does not show much of the power of that figure. Few subjects of discourse can be less grateful than the subject of Ineffability, especially when the narrator and the Speechless One are proposed as the same person. As soon as we reflect that the author has written a new text, we cease to credit his assertions regarding the perfection of his experience. He must have been exaggerating, we think, else his silence would have been the genuine silence of Johnson. Yet from the contradiction between a text that consists of protesting that it should not exist, and the existence of that text, we can at least draw this conclusion, that praeteritio is no less "a departure from reality and truth" than hyperbole. If the departure is harder to conceal in the case of praeteritio, it is because the reader whose enthusiasm is required will be put off by any author who, slightly or momentarily deficient in art, appears to be boasting about his reticence.

III. *Oeuvres complètes*, pp. 299-302

The theme of the sublime as theater is resumed in the article on *Hamlet* of 1886. It begins:

> Loin de tout, la Nature, en automne, prépare son Théâtre, sublime et pur, attendant pour éclairer dans la solitude, de significatifs prestiges, que l'unique oeil lucide qui en puisse pénétrer le sens (notoire, le destin de l'homme), un Poète, soit rappelé à des plaisirs et à des soucis médiocres.

In the following paragraphs the Poet reports the transfer of his attention from the "théâtre des nuées et de la vérité" to that which is enacted—whether in emulation or in spite of the former we shall attempt to say—"sur des planches," and in particular to *Hamlet*, "la pièce . . . par excellence." To inquire what are the affinities between this well-wrought product of "le seul théâtre de notre esprit, prototype du reste," and the peformances of the theater of nature, would be to leave the track of greatest interest. The tendency of the following discussion is rather to show, that, although they both attain to a "sublime" height of abstraction, the human play works out the theme of "le destin de l'homme" by an utterly different course from that pursued by nature.

It is in their abstraction from the qualifying influence of each other that Hamlet (the subject) and nature (the object) are sublime. The sense of nature's performance would be vitiated by human interpretation, for nature's contribution to that "sens" (the absolute otherness of nature to man) is nature's own perfect objectivity. The "significatifs prestiges" cannot be enacted until there is no human audience to misunderstand them[15]; their significance, from a human point of view, must be thrown away, if it is to betoken the sublimity and purity of nature. For this reason we are told, on page 300, that the "splendeurs d'un holocauste d'année élargi à tous les temps" amounts to a "sacre *vain*" (italics added): the sanctitity of the rite is contingent on the absence of spectators.[16]

Mallarmé faces the same problem of establishing his narrative bona fides that he faced in the "Symphonie littéraire." But here, as a reporter of what he cannot have witnessed, he has an easier time of it than he had there, as a reporter of what he *had* witnessed. This narrator can report without straining the reader's credulity, that the Poet, whose status as a subject bars him from the theater of nature where the objective world is absolute unto itself, can still bend his "oeil lucide" inward, until, in Kant's words, he "finds the absolutely great . . . in the proper estate of the Subject." The Poet can then *suppose* that the other side of the same absolute greatness is represented with equal fidelity by nature when nature is alone. In the expansion of the phrase "le destin de l'homme" to "l'antagonisme de rêve chez l'homme avec les fatalités à son existence départies par le malheur," we are entitled to see not only the ruin of the idealist at the court of Elsinore, but the predicament of the subject who discovers an augury of his own dissolution in the failure of the year and the setting of the sun. Hence the poignancy of the word "toujours" in the phrase "l'horizon pourpre, violet, rose et toujours or." The same faculty of abstraction which enables the Poet to derive an idea of perpetual glory from the image of decay, also compels him to interpret that image as a *memento mori*.

The parity of man and nature with respect to the absolute is elegantly conveyed by the reference to "prestiges." Littré gives two literal definitions of this word: "Illusion attribuée aux sortilèges" and "Illusions produites par des moyens naturels." The first of these senses is as active as the second in Mallarmé's paragraph, where the verbs "préparer" and "attendre" confirm the personifying effect of the majuscule in "Nature". Yet Nature is not the sole officiator at the altar of the absolute. Littré's third, figurative definition is also indicated: a "prestige" is an "Illusion produite sur l'esprit par les productions des lettres et des arts."[17] That the command of such "prestiges" is attributed not only to Shakespeare, but to Hamlet himself, is made clear by the description of the latter as "le beau démon" who surpasses the "maîtres-artistes" in power of conjuration; and of the actor who portrays him as a "souverain . . . de l'art."[18] It is emblematic of Hamlet's formal importance in Mallarmé's scheme, however, that his power to adumbrate "je ne sais quel effacement subtil et fané et d'imagerie de jadis" should be traceable to his mere "présence," rather than to any deeds of his. Just as the objective world's play-acting of the absolute was only a successful illusion when there was no subject present to witness it, so Hamlet's connection with the absolute—his custody of "la prime sagesse"—requires that he turn his back on the world. As the epitome of the subject he must abstract himself from every object. Mallarmé follows Charles Lamb, the originator of the view that Shakespeare's plays are less at home on the boards than in the mind,[19] by emphasizing the inwardness of Hamlet's "tragédie intime et occulte," "Son solitaire drame." The "seigneur latent qui ne peut devenir" is the exemplification *à souhait* of Mallarmé's self-reflecting artist; and in no respect more so than in his failure to produce any works of art (that is, any proofs of imperfection). Hamlet's very appearance on stage is such as to make him as little as possible an *object* of attention. Unlike the voluble "marionnettes . . . vaines [et] splendides" of our first passage, he wears an "inky cloak" that absorbs the light.[20] In his capacity as perfect subject, he is, so to speak, a Black Hole in the world of objects—or more exactly, in the center of the "espace doré et quasi moral" that is the stage. The action flows through him without changing him, as the other characters revolve around him[21] without shaking his resolution to "fix[er] en dedans les yeux sur une image de soi qu'il y garde intacte . . . sous le désastre."

Is there, then, no question of the poet's acting "in emulation or in spite" of nature? Has he no cause to begrudge the world the prerogative of the object with respect to the absolute, enjoying as he does the equally advantageous prerogative of the subject? Such is the opinion of at least one critic,[22] in which, however, our reading of two lines in the present text forbids us to concur. The first of these is Mallarmé's explanation of his readiness to withdraw from the scene of nature on which a drama of absolute significance is about to unfold: "ce n'est plus ou pas encore l'heure extraordinaire." The second is his description of Hamlet's career (the career of the man "qui ne peut devenir") as the "prolonge[ment] . . . d'un acte inachevé." From these lines it is fair to infer that Hamlet, the subject, and nature, the object, are divided by their common subordination to time and space—to the infrangible laws governing physical existence. The misfortune of this subordination is marked, in the case of nature, by the reference to "l'amertume feuille-morte," and in Hamlet's case, by the word "désastre." Hamlet and the world are strangers to each other in the degree that they are both removed from absolute Being.

Here, as in the two preceding texts, the word "sublime" is used to describe an effect of art or nature inferior to the effect of some act, or to the attainment of some condition, which is the narrator's main concern. It is used to describe the circumstances of that act or the preparation for that condition. In the first text, the "Théâtre . . . sublime" was merely the setting for an anticipated disclosure of "virtual" perfection; in the second, the narrator's beatitude was brought about by a "lecture *trop* sublime" (italics added). In the first paragraph of this text, the Poet is allowed to witness the sublime preparations for Nature's performance, but not the performance itself: the epiphany of the absolute through the object will only take place when he (the subject) is gone. At the Théâtre-Français he encounters the same problem in its converse form. There he views the subject (that repository of an absolute "joyau") from the outside only, as the latter struggles in a world of objects—"a sea of troubles." He is not permitted to gaze upon the "joyau" itself. The drama he witnesses is indeed sublime, both according to the definition outlined in chapter ten,[23] and according to Mallarmé, so far as can be inferred from his satisfaction at proceeding to a spectacle of which he does not use the word "sublime," from one of which he does. But in the vocabulary of a writer so preoccupied with a perfection that he cannot know, the word signifying the highest experience that human life affords is but faint praise.

IV. *Oeuvres complètes*, pp. 330-333

Several of the themes already mentioned are taken up again in "Solennité" (1887), where two forms of the word "sublime" appear. There is a reference to "[les] jeux sublimités [de] la Poésie" in the second paragraph (which introduces an attack on a playwright named Ponce), and, in the fifth paragraph, a description of the forces that can raise poetic language to "un nouvel état, sublime." Between them the contexts of the two phrases relate the sublime to the themes of the theater and the absolute; to the principles of irony and enthusiasm; and to the concept of "le Vers."

The context of the first phrase can be put as follows: the writer prides himself on his incompetence to speak of other matters than the absolute; he is incompetent, for instance, to decide which of two mountebanks is the more deplorable: the one who lays no claims to producing the effects of high art, who is satisfied to give his audience their money's worth of entertainment, and makes no secret of his venality; or the one who does lay the claim but cannot make it good; whose powers are not adequate to the task he undertakes; who affronts his audience, and the ideal itself, by "talking big." Mallarmé's dandyism is gratified by his inability to decide whether the impudent party does more mischief than the presumptuous one; but this choice of evils, and the patient philosophy that he derives from it, are interesting to us only as they lead him to mention "la Poésie, ses jeux sublimités" (*sic*). We have already noticed that Mallarmé's treatment of language resembles the physical process of sublimation in the metaphorical sense that he attempts to raise his linguistic material from the "état brut" to the "état essentiel." This argument here finds a striking confirmation in his use of the word "sublimités." The past participle of the verb "sublimer" (meaning to sublimate or to sublime) is "sublimé." "Sublimité," on the other hand, exists only as a noun (meaning sublimity). Yet "sublimités" is not employed here as a noun in apposition to "jeux"; rather, it modifies "jeux." The use of a nominal derivative from the root *sublimare* which has specifically literary connotations, in a context requiring the presence of a past participle to denote the transformation of "jeux" (*sublimés*), must be regarded as a deliberate departure from grammar serving the stylistic purpose of *identifying* the physical process of sublimation with the literary practice of the sublime.

Also notable as a confirmation of our remarks about the disinterestedness of the artist and the nonutility of art in Mallarmé's view, is the occurrence of the word "jeux." The "jeux sublimités" of poetry, like all forms of play, are by definition an end in themselves. The influence of the idea of play is also felt in the identification, at the end of this paragraph, of the substantive "la Poésie" (which it was not absolutely necessary to regard as a personification) with "cette déité" (which must be so regarded): the notion of divine play has caused the abstraction with which the text began ("l'absolu") to be transformed into a player. There is a considerable gain in interest in the fifth paragraph, where the first personification is supplemented by another, "le Vers," and a dramatic action is described:

> Que tout poème composé autrement qu'en vue d'obéir au vieux génie du vers, n'en est pas un . . . On a pu, antérieurement à l'invitation de la rime ici extraordinaire [i.e. dans *Le Forgeron* de Théodore de Banville][24] parce qu'elle ne fait qu'un avec l'alexandrin qui . . . semble par elle dévoré tout

> entier comme si cette fulgurante cause de délice y triomphait jusqu'à l'initiale syllabe; on a pu posséder et établir une notion du concept à traiter, mais indéniablement pour l'oublier dans sa façon ordinaire et se livrer ensuite à la seule *dialectique du Vers.* Lui en rival jaloux, auquel le songeur cède la maîtrise, il ressuscite au degré glorieux ce qui, tout sûr, philosophique, imaginatif et éclatant que ce fût, comme dans le cas présent, une vision céleste de l'humanité! ne resterait, à son défaut que les plus beaux discours émanés de quelque bouche. A travers un nouvel état, sublime, il y a recommencement des conditions ainsi que des matériaux de la pensée sis naturellement pour un devoir de prose: comme des vocables eux-mêmes, après cette différence et l'essor au-delà, atteignant leur vertu. (Italics added.)

We should not dwell on the element of personification in this passage, had we not already noticed the repeated association, in Mallarmé's prose, of the sublime and the theater. The characterization of "le Vers" as the "rival jaloux" of human invention, emancipating pale Discourse from her servitude to the latter—wresting her from him by the *droït de seigneur* and creating her his consort, Poetry—this characterization and this melodrama might easily be taken for a mere vignette around the points of real interest. But it is not altogether so. The behavior of the players, and their status relative to each other, provide a control for the testing of a general analysis of the passage. The attribution to rhyme, for example, of the power to "triomph[er] jusqu'à l'initiale syllabe," recalling Jean-Pierre Richard's remark that "à la fois radicale et finale, la rime figure pour Mallarmé comme la source et le couronnement fleuri du vers," is perhaps in itself a sufficient ground for maintaining, that Mallarmé regarded rhyme as the soul of verse; that the absolute value and "eternal" status of poetry in his thinking were directly conferred by rhyme. It might be a sufficient ground; but it looks stronger when we also observe, that in this text, Poetry and Verse, as embodied in the rhyming couplets of *Le Forgeron*, are represented as deities.

Another detail in the passage functions simultaneously as a part of the melodrama and as an independent illustration of the author's thought. This is the phrase: "*avant* le heurt d'aile brusque et l'emportement" (italics added). The fact that this phrase occurs *before* the actions of the jealous rival are described, encourages us to regard it as a sketch of the following abduction; yet the phrase is ostensibly presented only as a metaphor for the invigorating effect of rhyme on verse (or, of the reading of rhymed verse on the reader). Our awareness of its twofold function helps us to compare the phrase with one from our second passage: "le banal coup d'aile d'un enthousiasme humain." There, the author's intention was to celebrate the loftiest aesthetic experience by disparaging all experience beneath it. He attempted—with what indifferent success we have seen—to produce the effect of hyperbole by the treacherous and unwieldy means of praeteritio; and this tactic led him to protest, again and again, that his loyalties were entirely engaged on the side of the absolute. But here his intention is mainly expository, rather than mainly encomiastic. He has not adopted the strained rhetorical posture in which he had to condemn the expression of enthusiasm. Rather, he allows that such expression may be admirable in various ways ("sûr, philosophique, imaginatif," etc.), noting merely, that so long as it lacks the saving grace of Verse, it cannot be held to belong to the "répertoire idéal de tous temps," but is stamped as the transitory utterance of "quelque bouche." All that part of experience which he had put away from himself in the phrase "je ne jouis pas,"[25] he now explores for a "fulgurante cause de délice." Far from implying that the ideal and human speech are perfectly incompatible, he now suggests that the happiest result is obtained when the ideal (through the agency of Verse) acts upon the crude materials appropriate "pour un devoir de prose," and *raises* them (the first meaning of the Latin *sublimare*). He no longer pretends that he can dispense with those materials, or with the animal power behind the "coup d'aile." He no longer sets himself the impossible task of attaining the sublime without enthusiasm.

A moment's thought will reveal how *le Vers*, and more particularly *la rime*, serves the corrective function of irony here. Rhyme is ironic in the simple sense that the end of every line requires the beginning of another, to rhyme with it. As Mallarmé says, it is a "dialectic," in which every conclusion is inconclusive; in which every "fulgurante cause de délice" renews the desire that it gratifies. Like the reader of Marlowe's hyperbole, who was encouraged to look beyond the vehicle of every metaphor, the reader of rhymed verse never has the impression of having reached a dead end; of having spent his enthusiasm on an unworthy object, or on a single line of discourse purporting to tell all. The dialectical pattern of verse involves the subject in an open-ended system of statement and reply that admits of no final emphasis, no definitive discharge of enthusiasm.

The text presents a paradox, however, which confirms the argument of our eleventh chapter respecting the contradiction between Mallarmé's theory and practice of poetry. The paradox is, that while *le Vers* operates by imposing the ironical structure of dialectic on discourse ("cette différence" between the enthusiastic *alazon* and the dispassionate *eiron*),[26] yet it also assumes for Mallarmé the aspect of a divine principle in which he places absolute faith ("auquel [il] cède la maîtrise"). The freethinking derider of conventional religion bestows his "enthusiasm sealed off from doubt" in the only quarter acceptable to him: in the very principle of systematic doubt! Thus the indefinite postponement of the end which is the practice of verse, becomes an end in itself, *le Vers*. In no other way can Mallarmé circumvent his own profound skepticism and endue, so to speak, the robes of the hierophant that best please the dandy, than by making a religion of his art.

Mallarmé's faith in the divinity of *le Vers* enables him to unite the extremes of height and depth which unqualified irony would put asunder. This is the implication of his remark, that "une vision *céleste* de l'*humanité* ne resterait à son défaut que les plus beaux discours émanés de quelque bouche" (italics added), and of the image of "l'essor au-delà." In chapter ten we established that the simultaneous occupation of vantage points inferior and superior to the world of phenomena was a necessary condition for the experience of the sublime; and now, by the shorthand method of underscoring, we have suggested that according to Mallarmé, the poet and his audience must perform a psychological gymnastic of just this kind before they can enter upon "un nouvel état, sublime." His use of the word is idiosyncratic, however, in that it denotes the mere state of readiness for greater achievements. He does not regard the sublime as the ultimate aesthetic experience, but as the "recommencement des conditions [et] des matériaux de la pensée." Once he has caused the vocables to "atteindre leur vertu," he has still to combine them in new forms.

> Ainsi lancé de soi le principe qui n'est—que le Vers! attire non moins que dégage pour son épanouissement (l'instant qu'ils y brillent et meurent dans une fleur rapide, sur quelque transparence comme d'éther) les mille éléments de beauté pressés d'accourir et de s'ordonner dans leur valeur essentielle.

This image of sudden *épanouissement*—of an instantaneous revelation that is past in the very moment it occurs—we shall find repeated in the eighth and tenth passages discussed below. At present, however, before gathering more information about Mallarmé's conception of the sublime, we can only assert what we shall soon be in a position to prove: that this type of image (or more precisely, this amalgam of image and intellectual abstraction) is the result of Mallarmé's attempt to represent the ideal (which by definition cannot be represented).

V. *Oeuvres complètes*, pp. 375–376

Again, in the "Etalages" section (1892) of "Quant au Livre," a contrast is drawn between the measurable character of the sublime experience and the absolute character of poetry itself. A more occult expression of the same poignancy which his perception of this contrast led him to inject into the narrative tone of "Hamlet" is discernible here.

First, there is the author's familiar celebration of "le Vers, dispensateur, ordonnateur du jeu des pages, maître du livre." Now, however, the occasion is not the latest production of a classical masterpiece, but the "feuille hâtive ou vaste du journal." Readers who attached importance to the remarks in which Mallarmé expressed his lack of esteem for the manifestations of democracy,[27] will be surprised by his recommendation concerning newspapers: "plutôt que les bannir, occupation!" There follows an ingeniously illustrated defense of the proposal, that newspapers should be scanned for the presence of *le Vers* in them. Mallarmé argues that the press has always accorded a place of honor to the "traditionnel feuilleton," which

> en rez-de-chaussée longtemps soutint la masse du format entier: ainsi qu'aux avenues, sur le fragile magasin éblouissant, glaces à scintillation de bijoux ou par la nuance de tissus baignées, sûrement pose un immeuble lourd d'étages nombreux. Mieux, la fiction proprement dite . . . s'ébat au travers de "quotidiens" achalandés, triomphant à des lieux principaux, jusqu'au sommet; en déloge l'article de fond, ou d'actualité, apparu secondaire.

There is more than fancy, there is economic truth in the suggestion, that the upkeep of the city is paid by the traffic in luxury goods. But the poignancy mentioned in our last paragraph is felt by those who consider the source of Mallarmé's "leçon de quelque beauté" and reflect on what it must have cost him to propose it. For in the view, not only of the press and its artisans, but of Mallarmé himself, in his capacity of reader-for-information, the "secondary" importance of the "article . . . d'actualité" with respect to that of "la fiction proprement dite," is apparent rather than real ("apparu secondaire"). We are left to wonder that a theorist so strenuously pure in his devotion to an ideal of poetry should have wished to apologize for newspapers at all. And that we are right to wonder about this is confirmed in the remainder of the paragraph, by two indications of the narrator's dissatisfaction with the press as a forum for art.

> Telle aventure [of discovering literary merit in the "vulgaire placard crié" and the "texte politique"] laisse indifférents certains parce qu'imaginent-ils, à un peu plus ou moins de rareté et de sublime près dans le plaisir goûté par les gens, la situation se maintient quant à ce qui, seul, est précieux et haut, immesurablement et connu du nom de Poésie: elle, toujours restera exclue . . . du journal. . . . La notion prévaut, cependant, de quelque chose de très décisif, qui s'élabore [in the press]: comme avant une ère, un concours pour la fondation du Poème populaire moderne, tout au moins de *Mille et Une Nuits* innombrables: dont une majorité lisante soudain inventée s'émerveillera.

The writer is apparently of two minds. What is it about his attitude that excludes him from the group of "certains," to which no one might more plausibly be expected to belong? Not his opinion of the present state of the press. He is unlike the avid sifters "de rareté et sublime" only insofar as he looks forward to the imminent transfiguration of newspapers into a "Poème populaire moderne." To the degree that he expects this transfiguration, he is a mystic[28]; and to this degree the sublime is devalued relative to "Poésie." In none of the passages we have studied so far has this devaluation been so plainly made. The contrast of the sublime to the ideal is as striking as the contrast of the words "un peu plus ou moins" to the words "immesurablement" and "innombrables." Once the journalist's discourse has received the viaticum of *le Vers*, it becomes, as much as poetry, the "sort du temps." Here as elsewhere,[29] Mallarmé is preoccupied with the privileged moment in which the redaction does perfect justice to the conception. According to the argument of our eleventh chapter, however, he would best serve his own principles by regarding this moment as an hypothetical one. Instead, he takes the opposite course, the course of sheer enthusiasm: he expands the moment into an "era". In vain do we look for a sign, that his "departure from reality and truth" is a mere *gageure*, or the deliberate *reductio ad absurdum* of a jocular premise. The poignancy of the passage is in the breadth and enthusiasm of its divergence from the simple fact, that the anticipated era was never to arrive.

In what sense, then, is the author of two minds? If it could be shown that Mallarmé harbored no doubts when he declared, that "la situation" of poetry "se maintient"; that the ideal *in posse* becomes the ideal *in esse* on the page—then there would be no reason not to conclude, that he disregarded the sublime as a mere form of entropy—as the measure of disorder in a virtually perfect system. But we have also to reckon with the image of the "magasin éblouissant, glaces à scintillation de bijoux." That was anything but an abstract vehicle for the tenor of high literary art. Nor can the metaphor as a whole be seized upon as a proof of mysticism in the author—for it is not the actual contents of the store windows that he values, but their corruscation; not the jewels and precious fabrics themselves, but the way they flavor the light. Here he does not say that the literary text is unmeasurable. On the contrary, he implies that even in the least considerable opuscule, the presence of *le Vers* can be measured as if in carats. The metaphor is tantamount to a confession of his disappointment in mysticism. It subverts the hyperbole of the following passage by reminding us that any *Mille et Une Nuits* of the future will not be "innombrables," but the reverse. Each *Nuit* will be as real as a stone.

But when the delusions of hyperbole are pricked, the fortunes of the sublime begin to prosper. The measure of disorder is now seen to be the most valuable aspect of the system, in which the artist's conception of the ideal is but inefficiently transferred from his mind to the page. The sublime—the shadow of what was lost in the course of that transference—is no doubt less estimable than the lost quality itself, being merely "an inkling of what we know we cannot comprehend." If Mallarmé could rely with certainty on the reader's willingness to renounce the experience of the sublime, which is available to him, in favor of the experience of the ideal, which is not, he might reasonably conclude that, by comparing the sublime to its disadvantage with the ideal, he would produce an effect of cloyless enthusiasm akin to that of Marlovian hyperbole. To the extent that he actually evokes the sublime as the quality to be surpassed, he succeeds on the same principle as Marlowe, who, as we saw, invested the vehicle of every metaphor with a maximum of enthusiasm before revealing that he had something even greater in mind. In other words, he succeeds to the extent that the image of the "glaces à scintillation de bijoux" is sublime. But he fails to the extent that he seems to have no appetite for the contest, in which readers must scan the daily newspaper for "rareté et sublime"; to the extent, that is to say, that he lacks enthusiasm for any of the options of aesthetic possibility.

VI. *Oeuvres complètes*, pp. 366-367

The words "sublime" and "sublimité" appear at a remove of one paragraph from each other in "Crise de Vers" (1886-1892-1896). As was noticed at the beginning of this chapter, an interval of eight years separates the dates of composition of the two paragraphs in question. This dual usage, consequently, though it exhibits the other points of interest described below, is chiefly notable for the smoothness with which the transition from the first to the second form of the word is carried out. This smoothness represents the most important single proof of our assertion, that the word "sublime" is employed with remarkable consistency throughout the writings of Mallarmé.

In both cases, the word is coupled with an adjective to form an oxymoron. In the course of an exposition of his views concerning the nature of "l'oeuvre pure," Mallarmé has occasion to contrast the proper "ordonnance du livre de vers" with "cette unité artificielle" of the Parnassiens on the one hand, and "le sublime incohérent de la mise en page romantique" on the other. Now it might be objected, by those who recollect the drift of Burke's chapters on "Obscurity" and "The Cries of Animals," that the phrase "sublime incohérent" is in no sense an oxymoron. Incoherence, according to that Romantic work, is a cardinal feature of the rhetorical sublime. But that Mallarmé intends the adjective "incohérent" to function here as an ironic commentary on the misdirected enthusiasm of Romantic efforts to attain the sublime, is a proposition which the following sentence from another one of his articles should place beyond all doubt:

> Le poète idéal n'est point ce vaste épileptique que l'on nous dépeint échevelé, les yeux hagards, émettant indifféremment et d'un seul jet, sous *l'inspiration* de je ne sais quelle Muse bavarde, des vers faciles et incohérents, mais un penseur sérieux qui conçoit fortement et qui entoure ses conceptions d'images hardies et lentement ciselées.[30]

Inasmuch as the sublime is understood to refer to a literary quality, as opposed to a personal one, it is not, according to Mallarmé, a feature of the "mise en page romantique." The productions of authors who omit to consider their works with a measure of irony can be sublime only as testimonials to their enthusiasm. By the same token the "ideal poet's" conceptions are strong and permanent in the degree that he has shorn them of merely personal significance. At an early stage in the present study the terms "irony" and "enthusiasm" were selected from a multitude of roughly equivalent terms to denote the opposing principles that condition the subject's attitude to the object. We referred in particular to the aesthetic version of this attitude, in which the artist confronts an embodiment of the ideal that can always be regarded as a travesty. The doubt that attended our choice of terms is worth recalling now, because the context of the phrase "sublime incohérent" dispels it with satisfying finality. Mallarmé states very plainly, in the paragraph immediately preceding the one under review, that the aspiring poet's failure to hit the mark is ascribable to no other cause than his wayward pursuit of "la direction *personnelle enthousiaste* de la phrase" (italics added).

The limited and qualified sense in which we understand the second phrase ("l'obscure sublimité") to constitute an oxymoron must be carefully defined. We do not wish to discount the obvious objection to our assignment of the term, but to recognize the portion of truth in it. In chapter seven we adduced proof from two sources to show, that the precedent for associating the sublime with the theme of "brilliance" and "effluence" is no less authoritative than that which has established its better-known association with the theme of obscurity. So far as the latter association may have weighed with Mallarmé during the composition of the passage, the phrase "obscure sublimité" is not an oxymoron. On the contrary, it is a pleonasm. We do not need to be told that the sublime is obscure. The word "sublimité" being charged, however, with other associations than that of obscurity, another bias may have been put upon the phrase. The author is speaking of his experience "aux gradins des concerts"; and the consideration that readers would approve him for reminding them, that according to convention, those theatergoers among them who were not groundlings were gods, may have motivated the choice of "sublimité" (with its latent sense of *apotheosis*) as a paraphrase for "élévation." But the adjective "obscure" can only be seen as the dull half of an oxymoron if some firmer ground for ascribing to its partner the quality of brilliance is indicated. Such a ground is available in the following sentence of d'Alembert's, which appears under the heading "sublime" in Littré's *Dictionnaire de la langue française* (1863–1873) and may be taken as an illustration of the word's received meaning: "Je me pique . . . d'être ni aussi sublime que Platon, s'il est vrai qu'il soit aussi sublime qu'on le prétend, ni aussi obscur qu'il me paraît l'être."

It is hardly necessary to point out, that in the difference between the received meaning of any word, and the meaning it acquires from its context in a work of literary art, the whole dimension of style is to be found. But when all allowances have been made for Mallarmé's idiosyncratic use of the word "sublime" and for the insensible changes wrought in this, as in every element of language by the passage of a hundred years; and when counter-allowances have also been made for the sympathy with eighteenth-century attitudes that was so salient a feature of the Symbolist movement, both in France and in England,[31] then it still does not seem wrong to suggest, that as the microcontext of "sublimité," the adjective "obscure" must have struck the French reader of 1893 with greater surprise than its equivalent would have done his English contemporary.

It is well to diagnose the figure of oxymoron in this tentative way, because the force of our main argument concerning Mallarmé's valuation of the sublime speaks against the presence of that figure here. Only when the word "sublime" is intended to denote a superlative quality does a conflict with the theme of obscurity arise; for superlatives tend by their nature to converge on the image of a source of light.[32] But the case of "Crise de Vers" bears out the lesson of our five preceding commentaries, which was, that Mallarmé uses the word "sublime" to refer to the *circumstances* of a superlative revelation, rather than to the revelation itself. It refers specifically, here, to the mental atmosphere in which "le poème tu, aux blancs" takes form as an "éparpillement en frissons articulés proches de l'instrumentation." It will be convenient to treat this image (like the image of sudden *épanouissement* quoted earlier) as an adumbration of the more developed images of detonation and scattering contained in the next and final passages. This chapter, accordingly, will conclude with a description of the property common to all three passages of evoking the ideal by exercising the subject's imagination and his capacity for abstract reasoning simultaneously.

VII. *Oeuvres complètes*, pp. 481 and 549

The exordium of Mallarmé's lecture on Villiers de l'Isle-Adam contains a meditation on the theme, "Sait-on ce que c'est qu'écrire?" The question is addressed in terms at once vivid and astract—abstract, because it is immediately reformulated as a question of philosophy, as a description of the contest between the human spirit and the universe; and vivid, because the contest is represented as between elements in the real world having identifiable properties. Setting aside for a moment the imagery employed, we might summarize the metaphysics of the situation as follows. The act of writing is a means of palliating the misfortune of being forced to exist. It is the "ancienne et . . . jalouse pratique" by which one contrives to shrink the ineradicable fear that one is not in fact "là où l'on doit être." Were it not possible to write, "il y aurait duperie, à presque le suicide". The proper exercise of the freedom to write is not, therefore, in the service of the objective world, which mocks the subject by interposing itself be tween him and the absolute, but in the service of the subject's own capacity for idealism. He ought, like Hamlet, to shun the world, and "se retrancher" towards the "sens [qui] gît au mystère du coeur."[33] Yet it must be stressed that Mallarmé does not here overstep the bounds of the intellectual position outlined in chapter eleven. He does not vouchsafe any rash mystical utterances, but cleaves to his agnostic principles. The most acute inward scrutiny fails to descry the absolute; it attains only to "le mystère." The "riches postulats chiffrés" of poetry are not formalizations of absolute truth, but of "nos orgueils." Even the writer "qui . . . accomplit, intégralement" his spiritual self-vindication in the act of writing, must recognize that "an incertitude remains." So comprehensively pessimistic an outlook would suggest a parallel with the author of Ecclesiastes, if the violence and despair of that work were not tempered here, to a comfortable degree, by a conscious satisfaction in the possession of great literary powers.

It is not necessary to find in the author's famous *mot*, that the world already exists and does not need to be created again, a contradiction of his announcement in this lecture, that the poet's duty is to "tout recréer." As he observed in his portrait of Théodore de Banville, "la divine transposition, pour l'accomplissement de quoi existe l'homme, va du fait à l'idéal."[34] But if the poet cannot "*faire* des pierres précieuses"[35] by writing about them, yet his proper activity—the extracting of essences—requires him to maintain some intercourse with the world. The fourth paragraph of the present text does much to define the nature of this relationship, as will appear from the following sentences, edited for their imagery from the whole:

> Autant . . . que rien existe [*sic*] et soi, spécialement, au reflet de la divinité éparse: c'est, ce jeu insensé d'écrire, s'arroger, en vertu d'un doute—la goutte d'encre apparentée à la nuit sublime—quelque devoir de tout recréer. . . . Un à un, chacun de nos orgueils, les susciter . . .[:] une sommation au monde qu'il égale sa hantise à de riches postulats chiffrés . . . sur le papier blême de tant d'audace.

The paradox here is that, though the "transposition . . . du fait à l'idéal" is represented, both literally and figuratively, as a transposition of black and white—of darkness and clarity—yet this transposition, which should be the easiest of all to grasp, is in fact as incomprehensible, as "insensé," as the key statement: "rien existe." In other words, the paradox is between the literal and literary meanings of the passage.

The perfect symmetry that Mallarmé envisions between the ideal and the real—between the respective provinces of the subject and the object—can best be demonstrated by the supplemental use of other texts. The luminous relief of stars on the black field of heaven, for example ("la divinite *éparse*"), finds its man-made counterpart in the "ombre *éparse* en noirs caractères" mentioned in "Le Livre, instrument spirituel."[36] We can infer that "rien existe au *reflet* de la divinité éparse" not only in the sense that darkness becomes visible in Milton,[37] but also in the sense that reflections are always inversions (according to physics). A metaphor from photography suggests itself as a means of carrying this point. The disposition of light and shadow, of the real and the unreal, in natural creation, appears as the negative of their disposition in poetry. "La nuit" is sublime because it is the setting for the stars. They are something; it is nothing. But unlike the author of the universe, the poet (as Mallarmé observed in "L'Action restreinte") "n'écrit pas, lumineusement, sur champ obscur, l'alphabet des astres . . . [mais] poursuit noir sur blanc."[38] He cannot conjure any thing from the void, nor add a single particle to that which "existe déjà." His peculiar task is rather to derive an ideal product, that is, an unreal product,[39] from the world. In order to make nothing exist, he must use a real substance, "la goutte d'encre." Thus the inversion is cast in the starkest of oxymorons: the phrase "*rien existe* au reflet de la divinité éparse" may be read both affirmatively and negatively.[40] The stars, that are real and light, have a "sublime" setting that is unreal and dark ("la nuit"). The luminous experience of a poem, on the other hand, is unreal, in the sense of intangible, while the means of its production ("la goutte d'encre") is real and dark.

We have not far to look to discover, whence arises the "doute" that sets the writer's pen in motion: no farther than the words "nos orgueils." Here again, the symmetry of natural and poetic creation is completed by another text: by the description, at line seven of the sonnet beginning "Quand l'ombre menaça . . . ," of a constellation as an "orgueil menti par les ténèbres." Why should both the "riches postulats chiffrés" of human invention, that the poet traces in ink on the blenching page, and the natural counterparts of these tracings, the "guirlandes célèbres" of the night sky, be reproached with vanity? Surely because (as one might gather from a review of our discussion of "Hamlet") both inscriptions must take place in time—a necessity that confutes their common pretension to absolute status.[41] "La constellation . . . symbolis[e] le total qui est *en train de* se former," Gardner Davies has written; "les étoiles apparaissant dans le ciel . . . marquent la *formation progressive* d'un total."[42] Becoming, not Being, is the rubric under which every arrangement of ideas in words must likewise be classed. Mallarmé's symbolism of black and white in this lecture reminds us that neither the greatest of objects nor the purest of utterances is great or pure enough to escape definition as a compromise of the real with the unreal, or vice versa.

As a result of his emphasis on the divisive effect of time, however, Mallarmé appears to be teaching a negative lesson in the lecture on Villiers: the lesson that the wise poet is he who rids himself of the delusion, that his best effort to represent the ideal might not result (for once) in another relative failure, but in success. For a more enthusiastic treatment of the same philosophical problem—a treatment in which the divisive effect of time, though acknowledged, is presented as a surmountable difficulty—we must turn to the first paragraph of the "Préface à *Vathek*" (1865):

> Qui n'a regretté le manquement à une visée sublime de l'écrit en prose le plus riche et le plus agréable, travesti naguères comme par nous métamorphosé? Voile mis, pour les mieux faire apparaître, sur des abstractions politiques ou morales que les mousselines de l'Inde au XVIIIe siècle, quand régna le CONTE ORIENTAL; et, maintenant, selon la science, un tel genre suscite de la cendre authentique de

> l'histoire les cités avec les hommes, éternisé par le *Roman de la Momie* et *Salammbô*. Sauf en la *Tentation de Saint-Antoine*, un idéal mêlant époques et races dans une prodigieuse fête, comme l'éclair de l'Orient expiré, cherchez! sur des bouquins hors de mode aux feuillets desquels ne demeure de toute synthèse qu'effacement et anachronisme, flotte la nuée de parfums qui n'a pas tonné. . . . Peut-être qu'un songe serein et par notre fantaisie fait en vue de soi seule, atteint aux poèmes: or le rythme le transportera au-delà des jardins, des royaumes, des salles; là où l'aile de péris et de djinns fondue en le climat ne laisse de tout évanouissement voir que pureté éparse et diamant, comme les étoiles à midi.[43]

Two features of this text, illustrating points already made in this chapter, require to be noticed briefly. Mallarmé's insistence on the nonutility of art, on the independence of poetry from what Longinus called "questions of utility and profit," was considered at some length in chapter three. We later saw how that insistence was qualified by his enthusiastic recognition of the press's capacity to distribute literature on an unprecedented scale, with the result that he urged his own readers (and steeled himself) to examine the "vulgaire placard crié" and the "texte politique"[44] for signs of literary merit. Those earlier sections of our study now provide a gloss for the phrase "une visée sublime de l'écrit en prose." The sublime aim is defined implicitly, by contrast with the possible subordination of aesthetic concerns to political and moral abstractions on the one hand and to anthropology on the other, as an aim with no object but itself. That "écrit en prose" is sublime which has been evolved "par notre fantaisie *en vue de soi seule*." It is one of the "oeuvres . . . désintéressées, ce qui veut dire intéressantes," praised by Mallarmé in the first of our texts. The word "travesti" is doubly significant here. In the simpler of Littré's two definitions it refers to someone or something "qui a pris un vêtement lequel n'est pas du sexe ou de la condition," and in this sense it applies to the nonliterary "abstractions" that the *philosophes*, endeavoring (as Fénelon said) to "dorer la pilule," disguised beneath a "veil" of fine writing. But the verb "travestir" has also a purely aesthetic application, which Littré defines as to "changer un ouvrage sérieux en ouvrage burlesque." By implication, then, Mallarmé stands Longinus's conception of the sublime on its head: for according to the former, an "ouvrage sérieux" is one which has *no* "bearing on questions of utility and profit," while its trifling opposite (as represented in our sixth text by the references to "faits divers" and "articles de fond ou d'actualité") is concerned exclusively with such questions.

The other feature of this text that should be noticed in passing, is the reference to "le rythme." Like *le Vers* and *la rime* in our fourth text, *le rythme* may be understood in two ways: as an element of his work that the poet consciously controls[45]; and as an independent principle that makes itself felt in a given poem of its own accord, through the volitionless medium of the poet. (Mallarmé's textual change, noted on page 1601 of the Pléiade edition, from "leur rythme" to "le rythme," admirably describes this distinction between the subordinate and independent roles of rhythm.)[46] More interesting, however, than the dual nature of rhythm, is the literary effect which Mallarmé ascribes to its operation. That is the effect of causing a poem or an *écrit en prose* to strike the reader, not as a product of its time and its time only, but as an item in the "répertoire éternel de l'Idéal *de tout temps*" (italics added); as the "sort du temps." Within the compass of a single paragraph the author conveys a detailed impression of what he understands by this property, peculiar to the literary text, of transcending the limitations of time, by telling us first what such a text is *not* (in the description beginning "sur des bouquins hors de mode)," and then by telling us what the effect of such a text is *like* (in the images of the final lines).

The text that does not founder in time but that sums up all of time in its self-contained perfection—its little eternity—is a text which can neither be reproached with "effacement" nor with "anachronisme." The two failings are quite different. "Effacement" refers to an error of omission, "anachronisme" to one of commission. The author who renders the true lineaments of some point in time other than his own faintly, though without positive distortion, shows that he lacks the strength of mind necessary to render *any* point in time convincingly; for if time has proved an insurmountable obstacle to him in one case, it must prove so in every case. His evocation of yesterday will be faint in the same way (though in a lesser degree) as his evocation of antiquity. Indeed, his attempt to render the present moment must fail to catch its essence, there being no such thing (absolutely speaking) as the present moment.[47] Time will get the better of him in the time it takes him to complete a sentence or pick a word. He is in the position of the philosopher Heraclitus, who recognized that he could not step in the same river twice, or even once. His failure can be described in the terms of our ninth chapter (the terms of Kant) as a failure of the subject to exercise his innate capacity for conceiving an abstraction (that is, for creating an "eternal" work of art) greater than any temporal object (in this case, temporality itself). But the *effaceur*'s version of the past has at least the virtue of being not incorrect, whereas that of the anachronist, though vivid, is violently wrong. The former brings too little of himself, the latter too much of himself, to the vanished moment. The *effaceur* may be said to suffer from a form of the "similarity disorder" described by Jakobson in his article on aphasia, in the sense that he "spreads himself too thin" on the diachronic axis. His representation is deficient in signs of synchronic awareness: i.e. he fails to perceive the resemblance of all points in time to each other, and particularly the resemblance of the moment *about* which he is writing to the moment *in* which he is writing. The anachronist, on the other hand, fails to observe the difference between these moments: the difference imposed on reality by the diachronic passage of time. To put the distinction in our own favorite terms, we may say that the attitude of the *ef-*

faceur is characterized by an excess of irony, and that of the anachronist by an excess of enthusiasm. In order to create in language that "idéal mêlant époques et races" admired by Mallarmé, the writer must not allow himself to become so disengaged from the moment as the first *raté*, nor so deeply engaged in it as the second.

This paragraph belongs to the minority of passages relating to the sublime in Mallarmé, in which the author attempts to describe the ideal literary effect as he conceives it, rather than to the majority of passages in that class, in which the attempt at description is pointedly renounced. When the "visée sublime de l'écrit en prose" hits its mark, he tells us, it produces in the reader's mind the effect of a detonation.[48] The "nuée de parfums qui n'a pas tonnée" on the pages of inferior writers is suddenly discharged "comme l'éclair de l'Orient expiré." The specifications with respect to time and space in the last phrase need not concern us, for they pertain to Mallarmé's immediate project of introducing Beckford's Oriental fantasy. It is rather the image of the "éclair," modified as it arguably is by the adjective "expiré,"[49] that is interesting. As a metaphor consistent with the laws of physics, the image supports our contention that Mallarmé uses the word "sublime" to refer to the precondition for the experience of the ideal. It supports this contention insofar as we argued successfully for the common origin of the concepts of sublimation (in the sense of a physical transformation) and the sublime (as a term of aesthetics). Even if this "common origin" is considered to remain a mere postulate from the roots of words, the strength of the analogy between the laboratory process by which the tangible becomes intangible and the literary process by which the word "brut ou immédiat ici" becomes "là essentiel," [50] is not diminished. Mallarmé's treatment of this analogy, moreover, implies that he expected literature to surpass the sublime. The language of the *conte oriental* has already attained the elevated and intangible status of a "nuée de parfums." At whatever point one examines it, it appears to be the language of true literature. This is as much as to say that the *conte oriental* was written in a "sublime style," in the eighteenth-century sense of a tone of even loftiness. Yet because the *conte* serves an extraliterary purpose, because it is not an end in itself, its purified language sits inappropriately with it. *Zadig* and *Rasselas* are travesties of literature, according to Mallarmé, for in their case a mundane intention wears the language of disinterestedness. Such works as these appear to be fictions (that is, "oeuvres désintéressées . . . ce qui veut dire intéressantes"), but in fact they are written in order to instruct or edify the reader, and hence, to produce a social change. When the purpose of a work is less pure than its diction, the "nuée de parfums" will not discharge.

In the sense that Mallarmé understands the word, then, the sublime is a condition to be improved upon or transcended in the act of literary creation. His use of the word in this paragraph is fully consistent with his use of it in our first, third, fourth and sixth passages, where it referred to the circumstances or preparation for the experience of the ideal. We must now consider whether the description of the ideal literary experience contained in the final lines of this paragraph differs appreciably from the experience of the sublime as that was described by Kant and adapted for the purpose of literary analysis in chapter ten.

In one respect, at least, the lines conform to the model of Kant's "Analytic." They do not describe an object of sensation but the instant after the "évanouissement" of the object. Like the "éclair de l'Orient," the peri's wing is said to have vanished. The reader is not permitted to forget himself in the contemplation of an imposing object. Instead, he is forced to perform an act of intellectual distinction between an object that was present but that is absent. Now, if the lines were intended to bring the reader to a state of mind resembling that of Kant's subject in the third phase of the sublime moment, this act of intellectual distinction would conclude with the subject's recognition of his superiority to the matter of this, or any, representation, and with his abandonment of the text. That would have become irrelevant to the sublime pleasure of self-gratulation. In fact, however, the text does not lead to this result.

It produces instead (by means of the images of "pureté éparse et diamant, comme les étoiles à midi" and of "l'aile de péris et de djinns fondue en le climat") an effect in the reader's mind resembling the effect of the sequence of images in the texts from Joseph Conrad and William Cowper analyzed in chapter ten. Like those passages, Mallarmé's lines invite the reader—the subject—to experience the sublime consciousness of his superiority to the object of representation without compelling him to withdraw his attention from the text. It does this in two ways: by inserting a symbol of the subject into the representation (that is, by objectifying the subject in the shape of the peri or jinn); and by treating the natural element in the representation ("les étoiles à midi") in such a way as to exercise the reader's capacities for ironic perception and enthusiastic participation simultaneously.

To sanction the step of identifying the peri and the jinn with the poet (and at one remove, with the reading subject) it is not necessary to refer to the constancy of Mallarmé's use of the symbol of the wing. That symbolism has been explored in detail elsewhere.[51] The lines themselves contain all the information necessary to justify the identification. The peri and the jinn are races in the Persian and Muslim mythologies respectively, who resemble Mallarmé's poet in that they occupy a station superior to man but inferior to the angels. They are hyperbolizations of man: entities existing in an intangible *climat* (not the climate of the mind but of the natural world) who yet retain a corporeal form. They are the only figures in the entire paragraph; and they serve, furthermore, a creative function that is the natural world's exact equivalent of the poet's function in the intellectual sphere. Just as the passage of the poet's *plume* leaves behind it an "éparpillement en frissons articulés,"[52] of words, so the passage of the demigod's wing produces a diffuse scintillation "comme les étoiles à midi." To proceed from the identification of the peri with the poet to the identification of the peri with the subject in general and the reader in particular, is simply to proceed from a recognition of the poet's creative function to a recognition of the reader's re-creative function. Mallarmé explicitly recommended this step when he said, that "le lecteur, aussi, doit faire un effort" in order to know the "joie délicieuse de croire qu'il crée."[53]

When the subject has been raised symbolically to the level of a winged demigod, he has attained what Mallarmé understands by a sublime condition. The equivalent degree of elevation of the elements of the objective world is the level of the *climat*: the level of intangibility to which a "visée sublime" might aspire. What must be stressed, however, is that Mallarmé considers the peri (the subject represented as an object) and the *climat* (the represented object) sublime because they are ready to undergo a further transformation. "Sublime" is not a superlative term in his nomenclature, as we have seen. The absolute is only attained when the subject and the object, *having already been raised to a sublime degree*, merge with each other. This flashpoint of synthesis, at which the peri's wing melts into the atmosphere, must be of less duration than the briefest instant. It cannot be said to take place in time, because it is an absolute instant. Therefore we are not told that the synthesis occurs, but that it has already occurred: the verb *fondre* is in the past perfect tense. Yet although the synthesis cannot have taken place at any instant, it nevertheless must have taken place, since it leaves in its wake the "pureté éparse et diamant." The absolute itself is therefore technically absent from the representation; but the proof of the absolute is present.[54]

In the image of "les étoiles à midi" the text provides an excellent metaphor for the simultaneous absence and presence of the ideal. The stars are the greatest creations of the natural world; but because they are objects—albeit the greatest of objects—they have limitations of form. Their finiteness is perceptible in the fact of their distribution through space. So long as they remain stars, they cannot be divorced from their setting and foil: the "nuit sublime" of our seventh passage. To assert, as this text does, that the stars are present at noon, is to eliminate their objectivity—the formal component in their existence. It is to cause them, in other words, to cease to exist. The stars at noon are an imponderable abstraction: light with no formal source (so far as can be perceived) yet whose presence must be inferred from the net increase in sheer luminosity. Their absence is demonstrable; but so is their presence. "Les étoiles à midi" are therefore as much an intellectual abstraction as they are an image (so far as it is possible to distinguish between the meanings of those terms). The reader who attempts to imagine the stars at noon must posit a necessary absence: either that of "la nuit," whose formlessness would render the stars imaginable by restoring their form to them; or that of the stars themselves, in response to the assertion of their unimaginable presence at noon.[55]

This contradiction inherent in the vehicle of the metaphor is also to be found in its tenor, the "pureté éparse et diamant" that succeeds the disappearance of the wing. The two adjectives together suggest both the limitation of form and the transcendence of formal limitation. "Eparse" as applied to "pureté" need not evoke the notion of discontinuity, despite its origin in the verb "éparpiller." The phrase "pureté éparse" by itself suggests an idea of unified perfection as much as does the phrase "pureté diamant" by itself. But the notion of unity and self-sufficiency—of a whole from which nothing is omitted—is undermined by the conjunction of the two adjectives in a single phrase, and their further combination in a metaphor of which the other half contains words associated both with unity (*le midi*) and with diffusion (*les étoiles*).[56] Consequently one cannot decide whether to think of this "pureté" as a single flawless surface of limitless extent, like the surface of an infinite (because an insubstantial) diamond, or as an aggregation of points of purity separated from one another by areas presumably less pure. The first possibility is beyond the "province of the imagination," as Kant understood it. The words "limitless extent" denote only an abstraction. The second possibility is at least imaginable, but only if the "points of purity" are converted into units of form and the aggregation conceived as a scattering (of stars or diamonds). When this is done, the abstract notion of infinite unity is not being entertained. Purity has become local and relative, and is mitigated by its necessary association—necessary for the exercise of the imagination—with the contrasting principle of impurity.

This text acts upon the reader, then, in approximately the same way as did the passages from Cowper's *The Task* and Conrad's "Youth" discussed in chapter ten. Because a symbol of the subject has been included in the representation of the object, the reader is not led to withdraw his attention from the text in order to appreciate his privileged relation to the absolute. An adequate conception of the absolute and of the subject's relation to it can be gathered from the elements of the text itself. When the peri's wing melts in the atmosphere, the result is presented in a form of words that is neither wholly abstract nor wholly imaginable, a form that exercises the reader's capacities both for irony and for enthusiasm. In our discussion of the English texts we referred to a "moment of discharge" when the separate claims of the subject and the object to a special connection with the absolute are both recognized by the former. The aptness of our metaphor is confirmed not only by this text, with its imagery of lightning and instantaneous melting, but also by the lines quoted at the ends of the fourth and sixth sections of this chapter. Those lines also described the instant at which the absolute is revealed as an instant of explosive discharge—in the first case as a sudden "éparpillement en frissons articulés" of language, in the second as "l'instant que [les mille éléments de beauté] brillent et meurent dans une fleur rapide, sur quelque transparence comme d'éther." The feature that distinguishes all three of these texts from Cowper's and Conrad's applications of the same principle is the use made in them of the idea of absence. The reader's attention is held to the text not only by his symbolic participation, through the figure of the peri, in the events described, but also by the necessity of evoking natural elements not actually included in the representation. As we have just shown, this technique has the effect of involving the reader in the pursuit of elusive natural symbols, with the result that (like the reader of Marlovian hyperbole) he never has the impression of having reached the end of the text—of having taken its full measure or sounded its full depth.

Chapter Thirteen

A Foreword to Further Inquiry: The Poems.

Our investigation of the sublime in Mallarmé has concentrated on the author's use of the sublime as a concept in his prose writings. This choice of focus was prompted by two considerations. First, there could be no objection to discussing a text in which the word "sublime" actually appears, in relation to other texts by other writers of other times in which it also appears. If we had decided to concentrate instead on the corpus of poetry, that nowhere contains an explicit reference to the sublime, it would have been much more difficult to defend our choice of this concept as an approach to Mallarmé. This, at least, we have done. The second consideration was more important. We had scarcely begun our survey of the literature of the sublime before we were able to observe the consistency with which essays *about* the sublime have blurred the distinction between analysis and illustration to become essays *in* the sublime. We saw this tendency first in Longinus, who becomes, as Boileau noted, "lui-même très-sublime . . . lorsqu'il parle du sublime"; and then in Burke, whose treatise, with its enthusiastic descriptions of nature and poetry, is from first to last an exercise in the effect which it examines.

Mallarmé is true to type in this respect: as a student of the sublime he is also a practitioner of the sublime. Several of the prose passages discussed in chapter twelve revealed features of imagery and rhetoric that entitled us to regard them as examples of the quality they mentioned. In every one of them we found an application of the author's dictum, that "le vers est partout dans la langue où il y a rythme,"[1] regardless of whether the words are disposed in paragraphs or in stanzas. As a possible focus for the second part of this study, therefore, the prose held twice the attraction of the poetry, for while yielding nothing in literary interest to the latter, its relevance to the general argument of part one could be pointed to in a word.

Nevertheless, in view of the fact that Mallarmé's critical writings are generally valued for the light they shed on his poetry, it is appropriate to end the essay with a sketch of the lines along which a separate examination of the sublime as a feature of the poetry might be conducted. To do this, it is first necessary to stress the main lesson of chapter twelve.

Mallarmé's use of the word "sublime" implies a different understanding of its meaning from the one which we arrived at in part one. Yet the criterion for the sublime which we proposed in chapter ten *is* met by certain passages in his prose. These passages contain effects (in terms of their reception by the reader) which are represented as being more than sublime—as being nothing less than ideal. We saw this most clearly in the last of the ten passages, where the old analogy between a sublime treatment of language and the physical process of sublimation was evoked with this notable difference, that the treatment of language was likened not merely to the transformation of a dense element into an insubstantial one, but rather to the detonation of elements already insubstantial—already sublime—in an instant of explosion. The distinctive feature of this explosion (and of the images from our fifth and eighth passages that likewise occurred in contexts implying their superiority, as manifestations of the absolute, to the images that bore the label "sublime") was that it appealed simultaneously to the intellect and the imagination. While the visual quality of the explosion allowed scope for an unreflecting—an enthusiastic—reading,[2] the presentation of the explosion as having taken place at no particular moment in time provided a paradox to engage the reader's powers of ironic reflection. In other words, this image-cum-abstraction conformed to the definition of the sublime propounded in chapter ten. It conceded enough power to the object to engross the imagination; but it presented the object in such a way as to make the subject recognize his own connection with the absolute—a connection that lies in his ability to transcend the imagination.[3]

Mallarmé's claims for the ideality of the images in question, then, may be regarded as hyperbole—as hyperbolizations of the sublime. That he presents the images hyperbolically does not detract from their efficiency as means of inducing the sublime experience; but this is not to accept them on their own terms, either, as artistic achievements beyond the pale of our definition. Hyperbole, after all, is not truth but an exaggeration of the truth. Its occurrence here may be traced to the strain of mysticism already noted in the works of this author: the strain of unrealistic expectation that the ideal can and shall be embodied, without loss of ideality, in a literary text. To isolate the sublime effects in the poetry, however, it is more important to remember the peculiar features of these images, than to dwell on the supererogatory claims to perfection and ideality made for them. These features, any or all of which may be found in a given poem, include:

—A presentation of natural symbols (such as night, the stars, the sky, the abyss) that renders them in some degree unimaginable, and that awakens the reader's faculty of abstraction by forcing him to posit a necessary absence (of another natural symbol, or of the subject, or of the ideal itself) in order to understand the poem;

—An indication, whether by some action of the subject as he is symbolized in the poem, or by some other means suggesting the sudden reconciliation of opposite extremes (such as an explosion or other discharge of energy), that the hostility between the subject and the object has been eliminated, and that the claims of both to a connection with the absolute have been recognized by the former;

—The use of rhetorical figures (such as litotes and praeteritio) that lead the reader to devote his enthusiasm to an appreciation of the irony of the representation, rather than to any significant element in the representation;

—Any other means of exercising the reader's capacities for ironic perception and enthusiastic participation simultaneously, with respect to some formidable object of representation;

—Any other means of dispelling the impression of a conflict between the subject and the object in which the object has the advantage;

—Any other means of bringing home to the subject a sense of his intimate connection with the absolute.

It is further necessary to observe, that the presence in a given poem of an image that could be used to produce the sublime experience, or that has been so used elsewhere, does not entitle one to assume that its function in the poem in question *is* to produce that experience. Other conditions must of course be met. By keeping this obvious point in mind one can eliminate from consideration certain poems that might otherwise embroil one, on the strength of their imagery, in irrelevant analysis. "L'Azur" and "Les Fenêtres" are poems of this type.

The use of *azur* as a symbol of the ideal is not unique to Mallarmé, but there is no need to cite parallel cases to establish it as the "couleur du Paradis"[4] and the "couleur de la réalité céleste ou spirituel,"[5] because the identification is made explicitly in both poems. The eponymous element of the poem "L'Azur" is qualified as "éternel" in the first line and paraphrased in the sixth stanza as "l'Idéal cruel." In "Les Fenêtres" the "azur bleu" is mentioned as the provenance of the "éternelles rosées/Que dore le matin chaste de l'Infini" in the seventh stanza. This shared symbolism is in fact all that justifies one critic's reference to the poems as "à la fois parallèles et divergents,"[6] since in the main they address quite different problems, or rather, they describe opposite ambitions: "la volonté de tourner l'épaule à la vie pour atteindre l'idéal" in the case of "Les Fenêtres," and "[l'aspiration] . . . à se perdre dans la vie journalière, à tourner l'épaule à l'idéal"[7] in the case of "L'Azur." But the centrality of this symbol in both poems produces nothing like the sublime experience. In "Les Fenêtres" the celestial vision of the fifth stanza gives way to a series of images recalling the spleen poems of *Les Fleurs du mal* and culiminating in the "vomissement impur de la Bêtise." "L'Azur" describes a variety of strategies (enumerated in simpler language in a letter to Cazalis of March 1864) for avoiding a confrontation with the ideal, the redoubtable irony of whose regard has an "atterrant" effect on the speaker.[8] Indeed, this poem, which ends with the exclamation "l'Azur!" four times repeated, illustrates the possible abortion of the sublime experience described by Weiskel as an "obsessive fixation" upon "signifiers [that] begin to crystallize too distinctly [and] stand out in sharp relief from the continuities which normally subdue them."[9] The fact that the words "l'Azur!" signify an undifferentiated object merely increases the probability that they will stand out in this way. The words lead forward, but only to themselves again, suggesting that the speaker's "hantise" has afflicted him with the aphasic similarity disorder described by Jakobson. This diagnosis[10] is in keeping, moreover, with the fact that the entire poem has traced the speaker's failure to leave the ground, either literally, in the course of his various *tentatives d'évasion*, or figuratively, by exerting his power of metaphorical invention (that prerogative of the subject) to such effect that the object might have ceased to sting him with its "sereine ironie."[11]

The author of a study of the sublime in Mallarmé's poetry, however, could turn to advantage the disappointment arising from a purely thematic approach to the poems. That disappointment confirms another lesson of our twelfth chapter, which was that when irony so predominates in a body of work as it does in Mallarmé's, and typically determines that the attempt to render the ideal in verse will lead to a bitter conclusion and an acknowledgment of failure—that in such a case, the more enthusiastic members of the canon are likely to be those in which the right blend of irony and enthusiasm is achieved.[12] An inquiry along thematic lines, then, will discover candidates for sublimity which have still to be assayed for the sufficient presence of enthusiasm. This test narrows the field considerably; and while it is obviously not advisable to proceed too far into the poems themselves in what is after all merely an introduction to further study, the following texts may be earmarked for consideration at some future date:

—The sonnet beginning "Quand l'ombre menaça de la fatale loi. . . ." Jean-Pierre Richard suggests that this is "le plus mallarméen peut-être de tous les poèmes de Mallarmé, car, dans un langage d'une paix et d'une splendeur uniques, il nous fait assister au drame chez lui central, celui de la mort d'un être et de la resurrection d'une conscience."[13] Resurrection is the operative word in Richard's description of this drama, a drama with obvious parallels to the subject's transition from the second to the third stage of consciousness in Kant's sublime moment. Unlike other poems, in which the same theme of artistic creation is developed with an emphasis on the poet's impotence (poems such as "Une dentelle s'abolit," which concludes with the verb *naître* in the past conditional tense: "on aurait pu naître"),[14] this sonnet ends with the triumph of the subject: "cette gloire enfin vérifiée, assurée d'elle-même, [qui] peut alors éclater dans les trois substantifs terminaux du poème: *astre, fête, génie*."[15]

—The "Hommage (à Richard Wagner)" and the "Toast funèbre (à Théophile Gautier)." These characteristically represent the pattern of death and transfiguration which is common to all the poems of the *Hommages et Tombeaux* group. Both poems begin under a pall cast by the fact of our mortality: the "silence déjà funèbre d'une moire" of the "Hommage" and the "heure commune et vile de la cendre" of the "Toast funèbre." Just as he did in the "Préface à *Vathek*," Mallarmé enlarges what was merely an oppressive object in Kant's model into the idea of one's own perishability as a created object. This idea is more terrible than the most terrible object because it portends a doom that cannot be avoided. The second stage is thus experienced in all its force in these poems; but so is the third stage, for they both proceed to a recognition of the subject's eternity through art: the "pourpre ivre et grand calice clair" of Gautier's poetry, that constitutes his "gloire impersonnelle,"[16] and the "sacre irradi[é]" by "le dieu Richard Wagner." "A bon droit," Richard observes, "Mallarmé a donc pu célébrer dans le tombeau l'emblème qui a transmué une 'fatalité' en un bonheur."[17]

—The "Prose (pour des Esseintes)." Eric Gans has traced the steps by which the reader of this poem is conducted to and from "le sommet de l'expérience, la rencontre avec les Idées" that occurs in the eighth stanza. The first movement, "celui de l'hyperbole," is felt as "l'expression d'un désir tendu à l'extrême vers son objet"; but this movement, with its self-evident parallels to the second stage of Kant's sublime moment, is duly corrected by another, "celui de l'ironie," which affords the reader an abstract conception of "la pure Forme."[18] The enthusiasm of the first movement is thus converted into the irony of the second, in the fashion described in detail in chapters eleven and twelve.

—The "Scène" of *Hérodiade.* More perhaps than any of his other works in dramatic form, the "Scène" exploits the possibilities for a dual presentation of the subject's rational and imaginative selves. This presentation, which we identified in the exchange from *Richard II* discussed in chapter ten, is apparent not only in the comments of the nurse on the speeches of her mistress, but also in Hérodiade's "dédoublement du moi"[19] into subjective and objective entities that are equally herself. Her various contradictory attributes are the outward signs of this double status: she is at once a child and a woman; a woman and a descendant of warriors; and the qualities of extreme cold and extreme heat both attach to her.[20] The effect of her presentation as the subject and the object—as a being simultaneously glacial and torrid—is of course to engage the reader's capacities for irony and enthusiasm; but the presentation is also interesting for the parallel it offers to the case of Sappho, one of whose odes, quoted in the tenth chapter of *Peri Hupsous,* elicits from Longinus the following remark:

> Are you not astonished at the way in which, *as though they were gone from her and belonged to another,* she at one and the same time calls up soul and body, ears, tongue, eyes, and color; how, *uniting opposites, she freezes while she burns,* is both out of her senses and in her right mind?[21]

Next to this may be set Richard's comment on Hérodiade's speech beginning:

> Le blond torrent de mes cheveux immaculés
> Quand il baigne mon corps solitaire *le glace*
> D'horreur (italics added):

"Ces cheveux sont à elle, mais ils ne sont plus elle tout à fait, ce qui lui permet de se sentir par eux baignée et caressée comme *de l'extérieur.*"[22] The fact that nearly two millennia elapsed between the writing of the first comment and the writing of the second, suggests more forcefully than further argument could do the reliability of this dramatic technique as a means of producing the sublime experience.

It goes without saying that this list, far from being comprehensive, indicates only a few salient instances of the sublime in Mallarmé's poetry. Close encounters with the ideal are by definition not easy to sustain; and it is therefore not surprising that the effect of the sublime should usually be produced (as Longinus observed) within the compass of a few words. Very numerous are the instances of "la sublimité mallarméenne"[23] that can be located in single lines or phrases; and these would necessarily slip through the mill of a study that took the integral texts of poems as its smallest unit of consideration. Consequently an adequate examination of the sublime in Mallarmé's poetry would require many pages of close analysis, and must remain the subject of a separate book.

Conclusion

The preliminary aim of this study was to evolve a working definition of the sublime. We began by recognizing the difficulty of attempting to devise a single definition that would accommodate the mutually contradictory definitions of all writers on this subject. If the word "sublime" really amounted to nothing more than what Kenneth Clark has called a "vague commendatory adjective,"[1] it would not have offered an adequate tool for the accomplishment of our larger aim, which was to compare the manifest presence of the sublime as a critical concept in Mallarmé's prose to those effects in his prose that qualify, according to our definition, as sublime.

We tried to show that all writings on the sublime, whether they referred to an effect of rhetoric or to a psychological condition brought about by the contemplation of natural spectacles, can be understood as representing an attitude to the ideal. This attitude we saw to be composed of irony and enthusiasm, in varying proportions. Without altogether renouncing the vocabulary of psychology or adopting the method of purely formal analysis, we proceeded to close readings of texts from Longinus, Johnson and his contemporaries, and the Romantics. This eclectic approach was chosen for its adaptability to the discussion of those writers—notably Johnson and Kant—who used the word "sublime" to refer primarily or exclusively to a nonliterary experience. We do not deny that the record of a nonliterary experience can be satisfactorily understood by the method of formal analysis. Our contenton was simply that, provided we should do no violence to the rules of reasonable argument, there was no compelling reason to adopt that method to explore a concept widely understood to refer to an experience not connected with the experience of literature. Nevertheless, our ultimate purpose being to apply the conclusions of our general discussion of the sublime to the writings of Mallarmé, we sought to ensure that the actual fabric of our argument in part one adhered as closely as possible to the linguistic contents of every text discussed. To this end we attempted, in chapters nine and ten, to translate the ideas of Kant into the terminology of Jakobson and Saussure.

The effect of enthusiasm we saw to be a tendency to assume that it is possible to represent the ideal adequately in language. We observed that the enthusiastic writers of the eighteenth century tended to use words as though they were in no degree less potent or impressive than their referents. This tendency coincided with a religious belief that God was fully present in the natural world. Objects of nature might be ideal, and so might the words that stand for those objects. The deficiency, not to say the bad faith of this view, we discovered by contrasting it to the purer religion and soberer respect for language of Dr. Johnson. The enthusiasts' equation of the sublime with the terrible suggested that, even for them, the ideality of God was not easily reducible to the level of an objective phenomenon.[2] The necessity for irony in any treatment of the ideal became apparent.

The limitations of discourse that enthusiasm disguises are revealed by irony. A practical result of ironic awareness we discovered in Longinus's recommendation that the speaker should temper his enthusiasm by considering how its expression might appear deficient to his audience. In chapter six we saw that Mallarmé's attunement to irony led him rather to address the metaphysical difficulty of writing about the ideal without religious faith than the social difficulty of avoiding the censure of an audience. Yet even in the program for a career of literary irony quoted in chapter six, we found a sign of the author's faith in the eternity of art—a faith that lay at the basis of his project for creating an "oeuvre pure." In chapter eleven we explored this contradiction between the irony of his method and the enthusiasm of his aim. Irony itself, we argued, as it occurs in the "dialectique du Vers," was promoted by the author to the status of a principle of faith, an ideal to be served with complete enthusiasm: *le Vers*.

Kant's "Analytic of the Sublime" provided a structural basis for the testing of our ideas about the literary effects of irony and enthusiasm. It describes how the subject, confronted by an object of tremendous proportions, overcomes the strain imposed on his imagination, and ceases to respect the pretentions of the object to absolute greatness, by comparing it to its disadvantage with his own abstract conception of the absolute. Translated into terms suitable for the discussion of literature, this means that the subject's enthusiasm for the absolute, that is the theme of a given representation, must be tempered by his ironical perception of the representation's shortcomings, its inherent limitations as a product of words. His sense at the conclusion of the sublime moment of having leapt from an inferior to a superior position with respect to the object, has tended to express itself in an imagery of height and depth, or of light and dark. These pairs of opposite qualities or conditions offer the materials for an imaginative projection of the subject's passage from the relatively narrow "province of the imagination" to the "whole province of the mind,"[3] in which the power of abstract reasoning plays a decisive role. The imagery of height and depth or light and dark must therefore not be treated in a strictly naturalistic fashion, since the enthusiastic play of the subject's imagination must give way to an ironic reflection on the inadequacy of the imagination to represent his connection with the absolute. Nevertheless, the imagery may be retained up to the point at which it vanishes in the act of comprehension (*Zusammenfassung*). This act, which crowns the sublime experience, results in a sudden unification of the poles of height and depth; or in a simultaneous appreciation of the concepts of being and non-being—of existence and ideality—as they are symbolized by images of light and dark. The sublime text conducts the reader, in other words, to a point at which he seems to stand both above and below the object of representation; or to a point, alternatively, at which the symbolic properties of light and dark assert themselves before his mind in a single instant, as though in a flash.

When we turned in chapter ten to consider the operation of irony and enthusiasm in readings from several authors, we were led to two discoveries of general value for the study of texts. First, in the figure of hyperbole we found an especially effective means of forestalling the response of irony to enthusiasm. By seeming to refer to something greater than the thing he names, the hyperbolist engages the full enthusiasm of the reader, whose potential inclination to reflect ironically on the hopelessness of attempting to evoke the ideal by a literal use of language is not aroused. Hyperbole, we suggested, is the rhetorical equivalent of Kant's subreption, i.e. the assumption by the object (in this case, the signifier) of a spurious appearance of ideality or infinitude, that must be discounted by the subject in the third phase of the sublime moment. Our other discovery was that it is possible to include a symbol of the subject in an aesthetic representation of objects calculated to engage the subject's enthusiasm. Such a symbol can enable the subject to appreciate his own claim, *qua* subject, to a privileged connection with the absolute, without requiring him, as Kant's model requires him, to intermit his respect (*Achtung*) for the object. We suggested that the subject's capacities for irony and enthusiasm can thus be exercised simultaneously; and we showed, in specific texts, how this technique had been used to this end.

Both of these discoveries proved to have a bearing on our discussion of Mallarmé's approach to the sublime. The preponderance of irony in his attitude to the objective world bore the literary result of a novel treatment of hyperbole. He did not adopt the classical procedure of directing the reader's "puissance d'enthousiasme" into a system of straightforward and open-ended representation. As a route to the sublime that procedure could not but fail to strand the reader in the unfulfilled second phase of the entire experience. Instead, he employed the figures of litotes and praeteritio to ensure that no part of speech in his discourse should strike the reader as an available focus and outlet for enthusiasm. The reader of a text that refuses to name things, or that implies the relative unimportance of what is named to what is not named, must devote his enthusiasm (if at all) to an appreciation of the irony of his experience of the text. Consequently he will be led, as Kant affirmed he must be led, to find "the absolutely great only in the proper estate of the Subject," rather than in any unit of signification.

The use of language to evoke the ideal, that is not imaginatively apprehensible (not being a thing) and that therefore cannot be signified, is an ironical use of language—a use of significant elements to signify nothing. Mallarmé's efforts in this vein had the incidental result (discussed in chapter eleven) of leading him to substitute an abstract obscurity, that arose unavoidably from his treatment of language, for the thematic obscurity of earlier writings on the sublime. In practice this meant that his texts might be no less obscure where they featured images of brilliance and clarity than where they referred to night or the abyss. His writings are also distinguished by their irony from those of the eighteenth- and nineteenth-century theorists of the sublime (and from

Longinus's treatise as that exhibits the so-called Romantic features examined in chapter two) in the following respect. The space devoted in them to the celebration of imposing objects is minimal. Enthusiasm is misdoubted before it can take hold, and is invariably qualified by irony. As a result, there are no paraphernalia of hurricanes and volcanoes,[4] and no tendency to bombast. The sublime occurs, both as a critical concept and as an aesthetic effect in his writings, in contexts of serenity or intimacy. It is never produced by reckless fulmination, but in sentences "lentement ciselées."

If the presentation of the ideal in Mallarmé had been purely ironic, however, we would not have been justified in regarding him as a practitioner of the sublime. To qualify as such, a measure of enthusiasm in necessary: a measure of faith in the possibility that art *might* do justice to the ideal, to counterbalance one's ironic perception of the impossibility of that task. In this respect, the second of our two discoveries in chapter ten was significant: for in the figure of the Poet, that appears in various avatars in the texts discussed in chapters twelve and thirteen,[5] Mallarmé allowed for the symbolic inclusion of the subject—the reader—in the representation of the object. Despite the irony that characterizes the Poet's *practice* of his art, he receives, as a *symbol* in Mallarmé's writings, the endorsement of pure enthusiasm. The author repeatedly attests his faith in the reality of the Poet's connection with the eternal and the absolute—a connection that was supposed to bear fruit in the shape of the ultimate Book. This faith, coupled with his technique of evoking a necessary absence in the representation both of the ideal and of the objective world, accounts for what was perhaps the most interesting discovery of our twelfth chapter, namely, that he uses the word "sublime" in a less than superlative sense, to describe the setting or preparation for the advent of the ideal—an advent that never, strictly speaking, takes place. In the last of the ten prose passages examined in that chapter we saw how the motives of irony and enthusiasm had been concerted to produce a poetic description that was neither wholly imaginable nor wholly abstract.

The distinctive features of Mallarmé's practice of the sublime in his prose writings were enumerated in chapter thirteen. (These included his use of absence as a means of engaging the reader's faculty of abstraction, and his tendency to present the sublime effects in his prose hyperbolically, as though they were more than sublime.) Chapter thirteen also contained a restatement of our reasons for limiting the scope of the present study to his prose; and concluded with an indication of the lines along which a future study of the poetry might be conducted.

One final observation of a general nature is suggested by Mallarmé's limited use of the word "sublime." The fact that the word appears only in his prose writings, where it is employed to denote the mere conditions or circumstances in which the absolute is revealed, suggests that he regarded the word as a tool of criticism having no place in the essential language of poetry. Yet we have shown that it is the passages in his prose and poetry where an attempt to *render* the absolute is made that are sublime: the instant of revelation itself, rather than the mere circumstances of the revelation. This *décalage* of the word "sublime" from the effect of sublimity in his writings, suggests that it is in the nature of the sublime experience to arise incidentally, as a by-product of the subject's foredoomed attempt[6] to comprehend the ideal—to express the ineffable—to attain the unattainable. That the sublime is the ultimate aesthetic experience is proved, paradoxically, by the fact that it occurs only when one realizes that one has failed to attain the ultimate. No sooner have we represented the greatest possible contrast of light and dark, or of height and depth, than we come to understand that these are relative properties referring to the real world—properties that in their most extreme embodiments are still less great than what we cannot represent but would prefer to know. No sooner have we invested our enthusiasm in a work of magnificent signification than we reflect, with irony, that we have forfeited our capacity to prefer something better. Yet in this recognition of our frailty we are led to appreciate the capacity at its true, inestimable value. The sublime, as Kant showed, is a negative experience, in which the subject, obedient to the dictates of his moral attitude, voluntarily immolates his imagination to his reason, and his pleasure in the real world to his respect for a principle of unreal perfection. This authority of the moral attitude suggests an axiom by which we might regulate in a practical way our own attempts to experience the sublime. By substituting the word "sublime" for the word "happiness" in Kant's famous prescription for moral conduct,[7] we reach the conclusion that we shall most often experience the sublime if we do not seek to experience it, but make ourselves worthy to do so.

Appendix

Translations of French Passages.

(Note: Where a choice between accuracy and grace arises, the following translations incline to accuracy.)

Page 17

That [desire of my contemporaries to distinguish between the use of language for practical and literary purposes] is all right for narration, instruction, even description—the more so in that each person might find it sufficient, for exchanging human thought, to take or to place a coin silently in someone else's hand. The elementary use of speech serves the universal function of *reportage* [with a play on the sense of *exchange*] to which, with the exception of literature, all the kinds of contemporary writing belong. [Note the author's characteristic violation of grammar in the unclear antecedent of *cela* and the lack of a full stop after *monnaie.* Compare the completely different English versions given by Keith Bosley, *Mallarmé: The Poems* (Harmondsworth: Penguin, 1977), 47, and Bradford Cook, *Mallarmé: Selected Prose Poems, Essays, and Letters* (Baltimore: Johns Hopkins Press, 1956), 42.]

Page 39

Yes, *I know it*, we are only vain forms of matter, but quite sublime to have invented God and our soul. So sublime, my friend, that I want to enjoy this spectacle of matter which knows that it exists and yet flings itself wildly into the Dream which it knows does not exist, celebrating the Soul and all the similar divine impressions which have been building up in us since the earliest times, and proclaiming these glorious lies before the Nothingness which is truth!

Page 50

Why should a splendid gush of thought or feeling, of a size to be reckoned with, a long sentence writ large, one line to a page, its parts distributed according to their relative importance, not keep the reader in suspense for the duration of the book, by calling on his power of enthusiasm?

Page 56

—Don't you think that was a sublime idea of Lady Diana Wynham's to suggest that I make documentaries about the allies of the Democratic Crusade?

—The idea was more than sublime, chief. It was even not half-bad!

Page 59

Hyperbole exaggerates things, not in order to deceive, but to give an idea of the truth, and by making incredible claims, to indicate what should really be believed [Fontanier].

The special reflexivity of hyperbole arises from the fact that the mind, in the act of reading, cannot grasp the meaning of the words without making a judgment about their referents. Hyperbole does not involve a transfer of meaning, but a commonsensical reservation about the degree to which its semantic content should be believed [Gans].

Page 101

It is one of those exceptional mornings when my spirit, miraculously cleansed of the drab twilights of everyday life, awakens in Paradise, too imbued with immortality to seek pleasure, but looking around itself with a simplicity that seems never to have known exile. Everything that surrounds me offers to adorn my purity; the sky [or heaven] itself does not contradict me, and its azure has even lost the irony of its beauty, which extends into the distance, adorably blue.

Page 103

So I have only to remain silent, not because I enjoy an ecstasy that is nearly passive, but because human utterance would be an error here; in the same way that the lake, beneath the motionless azure unstained even by the white moon of a summer morning, is content to reflect it with a mute admiration that would be brutally troubled by any murmur of delight. And yet, a tear gathers at the rim of my eye, a tear whose primitive diamonds do not attain to nobility. Is it a tear of exquisite delight? Or has everything divine and unearthly in me been summoned up, perhaps, like a perfume, by this too-sublime reading? From whatever source it is born, I let this tear, transparent as my lucid dream, attest that thanks to this poetry (born of itself, and having existed in the eternal repertory of the ageless Ideal before its modern emergence from the mind of the impeccable artist) a soul that despises the ordinary wing-thrust of human enthusiasm can reach *the highest pitch of serenity* where we are ravished by beauty.

Page 109

Far from everything, Nature, in autumn, prepares her theater, sublime and pure, waiting to illuminate in solitude [its] significant spells for the only discerning eye that could discover their meaning (notorious: man's fate), the Poet, to be called back to mediocre pleasures and concerns.

Page 114

Any poem composed for another purpose than that of obeying the ancient genius of verse, is not a poem. . . . Even before the invitation of rhyme, which is so extraordinary here [in *Le Forgeron*] because it is identical with the alexandrine which . . . it seems to consume entirely, as if that flashing source of delight triumphed right to the first syllable—we were able . . . to acquire and fix a notion of the concept to be treated [i.e. the theme of the play], but, undeniably, only in order to forget it in its ordinary sense and give ourselves up instead to the one and only dialectic of Verse. Like a jealous rival, to whom the thinker surrenders his authority, Verse invigorates to a glorious degree that which, however masterful, thoughtful, imaginative and dazzling (in the present case, a celestial vision of humanity!) would remain without it only the most beautiful of speeches to fall from somebody or other's lips. Through a new, sublime state there is renovation of the conditions and materials of thought naturally suited for a labor in prose, [a renovation] of the words themselves, attaining their virtue after this difference and the flight beyond.

Page 118

Thus launched out of itself, the principle which is only—Verse! attracts to itself, at the same time that it releases, in order to bloom (in the instant that they shine and die like an evanescent flower upon some etherial transparency) the thousand elements of beauty rushing to arrange themselves in their essential value.

Page 119

For a long time the traditional serial, on the ground floor as it were, underpropped the mass of the entire format; just as, on the avenue, a heavy building of many stories rests firmly on the fragile, shining shop where mirrors are bathed in the scintillation of jewels or the subtle shades of fabrics. Even better, fiction properly so called . . . disports itself through the medium of thriving "dailies," triumphing in the most important places, right up to the top, where it usurps the place of news and lead articles that come to seem of only secondary importance.

Such an adventure leaves some people indifferent because they imagine that, allowing for a little more or less rarity and sublimity in the pleasure people take, the situation is stable with regard to that which alone is precious and high: what is understood by the term poetry will always be excluded from the newspaper. . . . The idea is gaining ground, however, that something quite decisive is happening [in the press]: like a contest, on the eve of a new era, for the inauguration of a modern popular poem, or at the very least, an endless *Thousand and One Nights* at which a suddenly invented reading majority will marvel.

Page 123

The ideal poet is nothing like the picture of that giant, dishevelled, wild-eyed epileptic who spouts facile and incoherent verses indiscriminately and in a single burst through the *inspiration* of who knows what garrulous muse, but a serious thinker who surrounds his strong conceptions with bold and painstakingly sculptured images.

Page 127

Inasmuch as nothing exists (and oneself especially) in the reflection of the scattered divinity, this senseless game of *writing* is a matter of arrogating (on the strength of a doubt—the drop of ink related to sublime night) a certain duty to re-create everything. . . . To summon up each of our vanities, one by one, [and set them down as] rich ciphered postulates on the paper that blenches at so much audacity.

Page 129

Who has not regretted that the richest and most satisfying [type of] work in prose—a travesty which we have only recently transformed—lacked a sublime aim? Those Indian muslins of the eighteenth century, the heyday of the Oriental tale, were like a veil thrown over political and moral abstractions, to make them easier to apprehend. And now, as science would have it, such a genre, eternized in *The Novel of the Mummy* and *Salammbô*, raises cities and men out of the authentic dust of history. With the exception of *The Temptation of St. Anthony*, in which eras and races are ideally blended in a prodigious celebration suggesting the spent bolt of lightning of the East, one searches in vain [for evidence of such a sublime aim]. An undischarged cloud of perfumes floats over the outmoded books in whose pages the attempt at synthesis has left only faded or anachronistic traces. Perhaps a tranquil dream invented for its own sake by our fancy might rise to the level of a poem: rise, thanks to rhythm, above the gardens, the kingdoms, the great halls, to where the jinni and the peri's wing have melted in the atmosphere, leaving in the wake of their disappearance only a sparse and diamantine purity, like stars at noon.

Notes

Preface

1. Jules Brody, *Boileau and Longinus* (Geneva: Droz, 1958), 38.

2. W. P. Albrecht, *The Sublime Pleasures of Tragedy* (Lawrence: University of Kansas Press, 1975), 17.

3. Samuel H. Monk, *The Sublime: A Study of Critical Theories in XVIII-Century England* (New York: MLAA, 1935).

4. George Whalley, "Sublime," *Princeton Encyclopedia of Poetry and Poetics* (Princeton: Princeton University Press, 1974), 820.

5. Jean-Noël Pancrazi, *Mallarmé* (Paris: Hatier, 1973), 14: "La poésie mallarméenne réalise l'amalgame sublime du concret et de l'abstrait"; and Eric Gans, quoted in chapter thirteen, note 23.

Chapter One

1. J. S. Mill, "On Liberty," *Utilitarianism, Liberty and Representative Government* (London: Dent, 1947), 97.

2. An account of this influence is in A. G. Lehmann, *The Symbolist Aesthetic in France, 1885-1895* (Oxford: Basil Blackwell, 1968), 21-73.

4. M. H. Abrams, *The Mirror and the Lamp: Romantic Theory and the Critical Tradition* (London: Oxford University Press, 1953), 137.

5. Benedetto Croce, *Aesthetic as Science of Expression and General Linguistic*, translated by Douglass Ainslee (London: Macmillan, 1929), 90.

6. Stuart Ende, *Keats and the Sublime* (New Haven: Yale University Press, 1976), xvii.

7. Ernest Tuveson, "Space, Deity and the 'Natural' Sublime," *Modern Language Quarterly* 12 (1951), 38; Frederick Stover, " 'Sublime' as Applied to Nature," *Modern Language Notes* LXX (November 1955), 485.

8. Stover, 485.

9. Thomas De Quincey, "Milton," *Biographical and Historical Essays* (Boston: Houghton, 1880), 127.

10. Monk, p. 20.

11. Clarence DeWitt Thorpe, "Coleridge on the Sublime" in *Wordsworth and Coleridge: Studies in Honor of George McLean Harper*, edited by Earl L. Griggs (Princeton: Princeton University Press, 1939), 199.

12. *Unpublished Letters of Samuel Taylor Coleridge*, 2 vols., edited by E. L. Griggs (London and New Haven: Yale University Press, 1932, 1933), I; 154.

13. Ibid., II; 261-62.

Chapter Two

1. Russell observes that the author's use of examples from the Hebrew scriptures was most unusual in a rhetorician of his time and place. See Longinus, *On the Sublime*, edited and translated by D. A. Russell (Oxford: Oxford University Press, 1965), xi.

2. Abrams, 74.

3. Longinus. *On the Sublime* in *Classical Literary Criticism*, edited and translated by T. S. Dorsch (Harmondsworth: Penguin, 1965), 107, 109. All quotations from Longinus refer to this edition unless otherwise noted. The problem of identifying the author of *Peri Hupsous* is discussed in Brody, 9n, and in Russell, xi-xvi.

4. Abrams, 74.

5. *Letters of the Wordsworth Family from 1787 to 1855*, edited by William Knight (Boston: Ginn & Co., 1907), II; 250.

6. *Coleridge's Miscellaneous Criticism*, edited by T. M. Raynor (Cambridge: Cambridge University Press, 1936), 320.

7. Malcolm Ware, *Sublimity in the Novels of Ann Radcliffe* (Upsala: English Institute, 1963), 5.

8. Russell, xi.

9. Brody, 88.

10. Ibid., 37.

11. Longinus, 100.

12. Ibid.

13. J. S. Mill, "Thoughts on Poetry and Its Varieties," *Dissertations and Discussions*, series I (London: Parker, 1859), 57: "eloquence is heard; poetry is overheard." P. B. Shelley, "A Defence of Poetry," *Shelley's Literary and Philosophical Criticism*, edited by J. Shawcross (London: Milford, 1909), 153: "When composition begins, inspiration is already on the decline." E. A. Poe, "The

Poetic Principle," *Representative Selections*, edited by M. Alterton (New York: American Book Co., 1935), 389: "a poem is such only inasmuch as it intensely excites . . .; and all intense excitements are, through a psychal [*sic*] necessity, brief." Paul Verlaine, "Art poétique," line 21: "Prends l'éloquence et tords-lui son cou!"

14. Longinus, 107.

15. Ibid.

16. Ibid., 128 (italics added).

17. This term is not intended here to suggest the possible use of literature as a means of commemorating the author's life (or any aspect of his personal being) so much as the longevity bestowed on *any* text by the mere fact of its publication in quantity or in a permanent form.

18. Longinus, 126.

19. Ibid., 102, 107.

20. Ibid., 107.

21. It might be objected that to speak of the "artist's ideal" in connection with Longinus is to attribute to him a concept from the Romantic age. The objection is valid to the extent that Longinus was a conventional proponent of classical rhetoric; for as such he would have allowed for nothing unthinkable or inexpressible in the universe—nothing that could not be dealt with according to the rules. But while the conventional features of his treatise and of his conception of the ideal are stressed in our next chapter, the unclassical character of a good deal of his advice (including his recommendation that the rules be ignored when their observance would impede the orator's "highest flight") appears to sanction our use of the phrase, whose limited application, with respect to Longinus, is about to be defined.

Chapter Three

1. Longinus, 109.

2. Russell, xv.

3. Longinus, 123.

4. Ibid., 146.

5. Nicolas Boileau-Despréaux, *Oeuvres complètes*, edited by A. C. Gidel (Paris: Garnier, 1873), III; 437.

6. Alexander Pope, "An Essay on Criticism," *Poetical Works*, edited by Herbert Davy (Oxford: Oxford University Press, 1966), 83, line 680.

7. Longinus, 146-47.

8. Ibid., 147. Russell has "the spiritual greatness of god" without the majuscule.

9. Ibid., 146.

10. Ibid.

11. Ibid., 120, 121.

12. Ibid., 143, 145.

13. Ibid., 107.

14. Joseph Conrad, "Guy de Maupassant," *Notes on Life and Letters* (London: Dent, 1921), 31.

15. Stéphane Mallarmé, *Oeuvres complètes*, edited by H. Mondor and G. Jean-Aubry (Paris: Gallimard "Bibliothèque de la Pléiade," 1945), 368. For a translation of this and other foreign-language quotations, see appendix. This sentence originally appeared in the "Avant-dire au *Traité du verbe*" of René Ghil (Ibid., 857).

16. Longinus, 139.

17. Ibid.

18. Gerard Manley Hopkins, *Poems and Prose*, edited by W. H. Gardner (Harmondsworth: Penguin, 1963), 155-56.

19. "Ballets" and "Autre étude de danse," *Oeuvres complètes*, 303-309. Cf. Havelock Ellis, "The Art of Dancing," *The Dance of Life* (Boston: Houghton, 1923).

20. Longinus, 145.

21. Ibid.

22. Cf. Havelock Ellis, *Selected Essays* (London: Dent, 1966), 286: "Aloofness is essential to the beatific vision. If we entered its portals heaven would no longer be heaven."

23. William Hazlitt, "Sir Thomas Browne," *William Hazlitt, Essayist and Critic: Selections from His Writings*, edited by A. Ireland (London: Wayne, 1889), 187.

24. Longinus, 146.

25. Ibid., 108 (italics added).

26. Ibid., 146.

27. Ende, 19.

28. Longinus, 111.

29. *Letters of Samuel Taylor Coleridge*, edited by E. H. Coleridge (London: Heinemann, 1895), I; 200.

30. Griggs, I; 117.

31. De Quincey, "Milton," 125.

32. Russell, xi.

33. See Théodore A. Litman, *Le Sublime en France: 1660-1714* (Paris: Nizet, 1971), 141ff.

34. Quoted in Thorpe, 201, 210.

35. Mallarmé, *Oeuvres complètes*, 869.

36. Thomas Weiskel, *The Romantic Sublime: Studies in the Structure and Psychology of Transcendence* (Baltimore: Johns Hopkins University Press, 1976), 24.

Chapter Four

1. Samuel Johnson, *A Dictionary of the English Language* (1755).

2. Jean H. Hagstrum, *Samuel Johnson's Literary Criticism* (Chicago: University of Chicago Press, 1952), 144.

3. Ibid., 144.

4. William Hazlitt, "On Shakespeare's Comedy" in *Four Centuries of Shakespearean Criticism*, edited by Frank Kermode (New York: Avon, 1965), 221.

5. Quoted in Brody, 56, 91.

6. *Lives of the English Poets*, edited by G. B. Hill, 3 vols. (Oxford: Oxford University Press, 1907), I; 21.

7. Longinus, 143.

8. Stover, 487.

9. Stéphane Mallarmé, *Correspondance I: 1862–1871*, edited by Henri Mondor (Paris: NRF Gallimard, 1959), 137.

10. William Blake, "Annotations to Reynolds's *Discourses,*" *Complete Writings*, edited by Geoffrey Keynes (Oxford: Oxford University Press, 1972), 453.

11. Longinus, 143ff.

12. Ibid., 132.

13. *Oeuvres complètes*, 367.

14. Ibid., 381.

15. Claude Cuénot, "L'Origine des *Contes indiens,*" *Mercure de France* 288 (15 November 1938), 118.

16. Weiskel, 27.

17. An example of this is to be found in Episode XVII of Joyce's *Ulysses* (Harmondsworth: Penguin, 1971, esp. 626–58) which consists in part of an "exhaustive tabulation [of] Bloom's present physical environment" (J. I. M. Steward, *James Joyce*, [London: Longmans, 1957], 31.)

18. *Lives of the English Poets*, I; 177. Cf. Diderot, *Salon de 1767*: "Si au sublime du technique l'artiste flamand avait réuni le sublime de l'idéal, on lui élèverait des autels" (quoted in E. Littré, *Dictionnaire de la langue française* [Paris: Hachette, 1863–1873], IV; 2057).

19. *Lives of the English Poets*, I; 21.

20. This substitution is discussed in Weiskel, 22–26 and 38–47; and in chapter nine of this study.

21. *Lives of the English Poets*, I; 182.

22. *Rambler*, no. 137, *The Works of Samuel Johnson*, 9 vols. (Oxford: Oxford University Press, 1825), III; 147.

23. Ibid.

24. Hagstrum, 150.

25. *Lives of the English Poets*, I; 182.

26. *Correspondance I: 1862–1871*, 207.

Chapter Five

1. Joseph Addison, *The Spectator*, no. 412 (23 June 1712) and *Remarks on Several Parts of Italy* (London: J. Tonson, 1705); John Dennis, *The Advancement and Reformation of Modern Poetry* (London: R. Parker, 1701) and *The Grounds of Criticism in Poetry* in *Select Works* (London: J. Darby, 1718), II.

2. In addition to the works already cited, see Thomas R. Henn, *Longinus and English Criticism* (Cambridge: Cambridge University Press, 1934); Walter Hipple, *The Beautiful, the Sublime and the Pathetic in Eighteenth-Century British Aesthetic Theory* (Cambridge: Cambridge University Press, 1957); Christopher Hussey, *The Picturesque* (London and New York: Putnam's Sons, 1927); David B. Morris, *The Religious Sublime* (Lexington: University of Kentucky Press, 1972); Marjorie Nicolson, *Mountain Gloom and Mountain Glory: The Development of the Aesthetics of the Infinite* (New York: Norton, 1959); Charles Peake, *Poetry of the Landscape and the Night: Two Eighteenth-Century Traditions* (Columbia: University of South Carolina Press, 1967); Alfred Rosenberg, *Longinus in England bis zur Ende des 18. Jahrhunderts* (Weimar and Berlin, 1917); Theodore Wood, *The Word 'Sublime' and Its Context: 1650–1700* (The Hague: Mouton, 1972).

3. Nicolson, 273.

4. Ibid.

5. Weiskel, 14.

6. The phrase derives from Dennis's journal-letter, published 1693, quoted in Nicolson, 277: "The sense of all this produced different emotions in me, viz., a delightful Horrour, a terrible Joy, and at the same time, that I was infinitely pleas'd, I trembled."

7. See Jonathan Edwards, "Sinners in the Hands of an Angry God," *Basic Writings*, edited by O. E. Winslow (New York: New American Library, 1966), 150-67.

8. Weiskel, 84.

9. Ibid., 87.

10. Dennis, *Select Works*, I; 339.

11. A. C. Bradley, "The Sublime," *Oxford Lectures on Poetry* (London: Macmillan, 1909), 41-45.

12. Dennis, *Select Works*, II; 459-60.

13. Ibid., II; 438.

14. Ibid., I; 365.

15. J. S. Mill, *Three Essays on Religion* (London: Longmans, 1923), 90.

16. Ibid., 91.

17. *Correspondance I: 1862-1871*, 241.

18. A recent discussion of the *plumage*, which "forms part of a carefully constructed self-referential pattern . . . clearly established throughout his work," is in Timothy Hampton, "Virgil, Baudelaire and Mallarmé at the Sign of the Swan: Poetic Translation and Historical Allegory," *Romanic Review* 73; 4 (November 1982), 448.

19. Michael Riffaterre, "On Deciphering Mallarmé," *The Georgia Review* 29; 1 (1975), 85.

20. Quoted in Albrecht, p. 50.

21. Archibald Alison, *Essays on the Nature and Principles of Taste* (Edinburgh: Bell & Bradfute, 1790).

22. "The Character of Milton's Satan," *William Hazlitt: Essayist and Critic*, 118-20.

23. Tuveson, 31.

24. Coleridge, "Kubla Khan," line 12; Pascal, *Pensées*, section III, 206. Kant, on the other hand, maintained that "to take an immediate interest in the beauty of nature . . . is always a mark of a good soul." "Analytic of the Sublime," *The Critique of Judgment*, translated by J. C. Meredith (Oxford: Oxford University Press, 1969), 157.

25. *Letters of John Keats*, edited by M. B. Forman (Oxford: Oxford University Press, 1935), 31.

26. John Ruskin, *Modern Painters* (New York: J. Wiley, 1872), III; 295-98.

27. Edmund Burke, *A Philosophical Inquiry into the Origin of Our Ideas of the Sublime and Beautiful* in *The Works of the Right Honorable Edmund Burke*, 4th ed. (Boston: Little, Brown, 1871), I; 119.

28. Ibid.

29. The imprecision is convincing only so long as it is not noticed. The author is employing the figure of *ploce* or *antanaclasis* (i.e. a sequential play upon two meanings of the same word); but when the figure is detected, the speciousness of the argument becomes apparent.

30. Weiskel, 3.

31. *The Works of Samuel Johnson* (Oxford: Oxford University Press, 1825), VII; 213.

32. A detailed account of this movement (including critiques of works by Thomas Burnet, Joseph Addison, John Ray, and others) is in Marjorie Nicolson, *Mountain Gloom and Mountain Glory*, esp. 184-323.

33. *The Critical Works of John Dennis*, edited by E. N. Hooker (Baltimore: The Johns Hopkins Press, 1939-43), I; 365.

Chapter Six

1. Other names might have been given to the complementary principles mentioned here. If we have preferred enthusiasm and irony to wit and judgment, however, it is not only because the vocabulary of baroque aesthetics lies outside the province of this study, but because the consistency of their usage offers a convenient means of comparing verbatim the pronouncements of every thinker on the question of the sublime. The terms occur in Longinus, in the Augustan and Romantic critics, and in Mallarmé. Enthusiasm has the special advantage over its approximate synonyms of suggesting "a *vain* confidence of divine favour or communication" (Johnson's *Dictionary*, italics added). Mallarmé would imply that the vanity of this confidence makes itself felt in a descent from the divine to the brutish, or more accurately, in a recognition that the claim to omniscience proceeds from an unreflecting state of mind.

2. *Correspondance I: 1862-1871*, 207.

3. The opposition between these last two pairs is apparent when the religious point of view described in chapter four is recalled. When the ideal is conceived as Johnson conceived it, as the potential source of real benefits and punishments, then Truth and Glory are not to be equated with "le Rien" but ascribed to God. The Word is glorious, not the "mensonges" of the scribbler. The basic opposition is between the affirmative response of the enthusiast, and the denial of the ironist, with respect to the question whether the ideal can take a real or literary form.

4. This is not to say that a poem must not be sufficiently comprehensible for the reader to be able to recognize that it is *about* the ideal (i.e. that it is not sheer nonsense). Our statement points rather to the fundamental incompatibility between language and the ineffable — an incompatibility that in no sense forbids one to write *about* the ineffable.

5. Eric Gans, "Prose poétique," *Romanic Review* 66; 3 (1975), 187-98.

6. *The Journals and Notebooks of Ralph Waldo Emerson*, edited by A. W. Plumstead (Cambridge: Harvard University Press, 1969), VII; 303.

7. *Oeuvres complètes*, 869.

8. Mallarmé himself employs this metaphor in the excerpt from the "Avant-dire au *Traité du verbe*" quoted previously.

9. Letter to Cazalis, 14 May 1867 ("Ma pensée s'est pensée," etc.).

10. *The Works of Samuel Johnson*, I; 266.

11. *Letters of Samuel Taylor Coleridge*, 200.

12. *Webster's New Collegiate Dictionary* (Springfield: Merriam, 1951), 495.

13. Longinus, 109.

14. *Oeuvres complètes*, 663. Mallarmé regarded the natural creation as a category of subordinate importance to that of literary creation. "Les choses existent, nous n'avons pas à les créer" he told Jules Huret; and "tout, au monde, existe pour aboutir à un Livre." (Ibid., 871, 378.)

15. Here and in chapter eleven we argue the ambivalence of Mallarmé's attitude to the ideal. This interpretation is consistent with the tension which we shall notice in the texts discussed in chapter twelve, between the impulses ironically to deny and enthusiastically to affirm the possibility of writing about the ideal without "travestying" it. T. S. Eliot took a different view: "Poe et Mallarmé ont la passion de la spéculation métaphysique, mais il est évident qu'ils ne croient pas aux théories auxquelles ils s'intéressent ou qu'ils inventent. . . . Ils se servent de leurs théories pour . . . raffiner et développer leur puissance de sensibilité et d'émotion." ("Note sur Mallarmé et Poe," *Nouvelle Revue Française*, 11 [1926], 525.)

16. Remy de Gourmont, "Stéphane Mallarmé," *Selected Writings*, edited and translated by Glenn Burne (Ann Arbor: University of Michigan Press, 1966), 183.

17. Cf. Cuénot, "L'effort pour juxtaposer et non pour subordonner (le poète escamote les relatifs quand il peut)" (p. 118). Norman Paxton notes as characteristic features of Mallarmé's later prose style "the separation of elements which belong together" and "the piling up of nouns and adjectives, often stress[ed] . . . by the omission or ellipsis of the verb." (*The Development of Mallarmé's Prose Style* [Geneva: Droz, 1968], 51, 56.) A list of Mallarmé's characteristic departures from grammar is appended to Jacques Schérer's *Grammaire de Mallarmé* (Paris: Nizet, 1977), 248-49.

18. This description of his purpose is proposed only as an hypothesis for the comparative study outlined here. It might be argued to the contrary, that Christ used parables to translate the unknown truth of God into understandable, everyday terms, whereas the Symbolists harbored, in many cases, an avowedly obscurantist intention.

Chapter Seven

1. R. S. Crane, review of Monk, *The Sublime*, in *Philological Quarterly* 15; 2 (April 1936), 167; and Nicolson, p. 276n.

2. Longinus, 129.

3. J. S. Mill, *Autobiography* (London: Oxford University Press, 1924), 158.

4. Longinus, 141.

5. Mallarmé refers to a similar effect in "Le Démon de l'Analogie": "la suspension fatidique" between the end of one line of verse and the beginning of the next. (*Oeuvres complètes*, 272.)

6. That is, after the second term has been reached and found wanting (the ironical impulse having succeeded the enthusiastic one).

7. Abrams, 73.

8. Longinus, 132.

9. *Oeuvres complètes*, 381 (italics added).

10. Longinus, 127, 128, 139. The *Oxford English Dictionary* defines *effluence* as "A flowing out (esp. of light, [etc.]) . . . [as in] 'gladdened by that broad effluence of light.' "

11. Burke, 134.

12. Eric Gans, "Hyperbole et ironie," *Littérature* 24 (1975), 489.

13. This intention characteristically motivates what the same author elsewhere calls "l'expression d'un désir tendu à l'extrême vers son objet." ("Prose poétique," 193.)

14. Longinus, 123.

15. *William Hazlitt, Essayist and Critic,* 415.

16. Quoted in Thorpe, 215.

17. Quoted in Albrecht, 135.

18. Ware, 8 (italics added).

19. Vladimir Jankélévitch, *L'Ironie* (Paris: Flammarion, 1964), 163.

20. Abrams, 56.

Chapter Eight

1. Longinus, 106.

2. *The Works of Samuel Johnson,* VII; 259, 341.

3. Quoted in Abrams, 349.

4. Russell, xv.

5. Cf. Claude Abastado: "[Mallarmé] suggère . . . que 'c'est le lecteur qui doit être inspiré,' que le poème est l' 'instrument' de cette grâce reçue, et qu'enfin 'l'enthousiasme n'est pas un état d'âme d'écrivain aux heures de la création.' " *Expérience et théorie de la création poétique chez Mallarmé* (Paris: Archives des lettres modernes, 4; 119, 1970), 13.

6. Quoted in Brody, 89.

7. This is perhaps somewhat to overstate the position of the Romantics in the interest of distinguishing clearly between two possible or theoretical positions on the importance of facts in rhetoric. That the empirical tradition of the eighteenth century was prolonged through the nineteenth is observable not only in the sciences but in literature: the stories of Poe (1809–1849), for example, derive much of their power from the incorporation of plausible "scientific" detail.

8. Longinus, 150. If, however, we include the ancient phenomenon of the fool under the first of these headings, we are obliged to include the satirist under the second. The fool was a satirist unconsciously; the satirist is a charlatan masquerading as a fool.

9. Quoted in Herschel M. Sikes, "The Poetic Theory and Practice of Keats: the Record of a Debt to Hazlitt," *Philological Quarterly* 38; 4 (October 1954), 404.

10. William Wordsworth, "Fidelity," *Complete Poetical Works* (Boston: Houghton, 1904), 320–21.

11. Jankélévitch, 9.

12. Weiskel, 6.

13. John Ruskin, *Modern Painters* (New York: J. Wiley, 1872), vol. I, pt. 2, ch. 2.

14. See, for example, Sir Walter Scott, *The Antiquary* (London: Dent, 1977), ch. XVII, p. 154; *Rob Roy* (London: Dent, 1978), ch. XXXVI, p. 345; and Ann Radcliffe, *The Mysteries of Udolpho*, (London: Robinson, 1794), *passim*.

15. Jankélévitch, 35.

16. Plato, *Timaeus*, translated by Francis M. Cornford (Indianapolis: Bobbs-Merrill, 1959), sections 65C–85E.

17. Maurice Dekobra, *La Madone à Hollywood* (Paris: Baudinière, 1946), 67–68.

18. Algernon Swinburne, "Christopher Marlowe," *Swinburne as Critic*, edited by Clyde K. Hyder (London: Routledge, 1972), 278.

19. Christopher Marlowe, *The Tragical History of Doctor Faustus*, Act V, scene ii, lines 112–17.

20. C. S. Lewis, "Hero and Leander," *Selected Literary Essays*, edited by Walter Hooper (Cambridge: Cambridge University Press, 1979), 60.

21. T. S. Eliot, "Christopher Marlowe," *Essays on Elizabethan Drama* (New York: Harcourt, 1960), 58.

22. Pierre Fontanier, *Les Figures du discours* (Paris: Flammarion, 1968), 123–24.

23. "Hyperbole et ironie," 490.

24. Christopher Marlowe, *Tamburlaine the Great, Part One*, Act I, scene i, lines 25–31.

25. Longinus, 107.

26. This reason is of course also embodied in a text—in the sentence from Coleridge quoted immediately below. Our emphasis on the fact that it was enunciated at a particular moment in history is intended to recall the argument developed in chapter seven respecting the special favor in which hyperbole was held by the Romantics as opposed to the writers of other ages.

27. The definition is Michael Riffaterre's.

28. *The Complete Works of Samuel Taylor Coleridge*, edited by W. G. T. Shedd (New York: Harper, 1864), II; 337. Cf. Mme de Staël, quoted in Littré, vol. 4, p. 2057: "On n'arrive point au sublime par degrés; des distances infinies le séparent même de ce qui n'est que beau."

29. Quoted in the *Times Literary Supplement*, 10 July 1981, p. 783. Cf. Marmontel, quoted in Littré, vol. 4, p. 2057: "En général, le ridicule touche au sublime; et, pour marcher sur la limite qui les sépare, sans la passer jamais, il faut bien prendre garde à soi."

Chapter Nine

1. *Oeuvres complètes*, 272.

2. Gans, "Prose poétique," 197.

3. Ibid., 194.

4. Weiskel, 38.

5. Immanuel Kant, *Observations on the Feeling of the Beautiful and Sublime*, translated by John T. Goldthwait (Berkeley: University of California Press, 1960), 47-50.

6. Pertinent discussions are in Milton C. Nahm, " 'Sublimity' and the 'Moral Law' in Kant's Philosophy," *Kant-Studien* 48 (1956-57), 502-24; R. L. Zimmerman, "Kant: The Aesthetic Judgment," *Journal of Aesthetics and Art Criticism* (1962-63), 333-44; and Israel Knox, *The Aesthetic Theories of Kant, Hegel, and Schopenhauer* (New York: Humanities Press, 1958), 54-68.

7. Immanuel Kant, *Critique of Judgment*, translated by J. C. Meredith (Oxford: Oxford University Press, 1969), 13.

8. Ibid., 62.

9. This holds true for the literary experience of the sublime as well, since the reading of any text, as Roland Barthes points out, is "semelfactive" (i.e., it occurs only once). The experience of a text "can be repeated only as difference" ("From Work to Text," *Textual Strategies: Perspectives in Post-Structuralist Criticism*, edited by Josué V. Harari [Ithaca: Cornell University Press, 1979], 77).

10. Weiskel, 38.

11. Ibid., 23, 39.

12. "Analytic of the Sublime," 108.

13. Ibid., 106.

14. Weiskel, 39; "Analytic of the Sublime," 121.

15. Weiskel, 39.

16. "Analytic of the Sublime," 120.

17. Ibid., 118.

18. Weiskel, 41-42.

19. Ronald Crane, review of Monk, *The Sublime*, in *Philological Quarterly* 15; 2 (April 1936), 166.

20. Tuveson, 38n.

21. Ibid., 20.

22. Longinus, 118, 146, 147.

23. Nicolson, 30.

24. Albrecht, 34.

25. Paul Goodman, *The Structure of Literature* (Chicago: University of Chicago Press, 1954), 253–54.

26. Weiskel, 23.

27. Roman Jakobson, "Two Aspects of Language and Two Types of Aphasic Disturbances" in Jakobson and Morris Halle, *Fundamentals of Language* (The Hague: Mouton, 1956), 55–82.

28. Weiskel, 23.

29. Ibid., 26–27. Cf. Julia Kristeva: "L' 'objet' sublime se dissout dans les transports d'une mémoire sans fond. . . . Aussitôt que je le perçois . . . le sublime déclenche . . . une cascade de perceptions et de mots qui élargissent la mémoire à l'infini." *Pouvoirs de l'horreur: essai sur l'abjection* (Paris: Seuil, 1980), 19.

30. Weiskel, 28.

31. *Complete Poetical Works*, 463.

32. Weiskel, 29.

Chapter Ten

1. Burke, 130.

2. *The Table Talk and Omniana of Samuel Taylor Coleridge*, edited by T. Ashe (London: G. Bell, 1903), 73. Bradley, 53–54, refers to "Burke's general doctrine (a doctrine impossible to accept)."

3. Our use of the term "signified" as an approximate synonym

for "image" is open to question. While the imagistic strains in Saussure's definition appear to support it, later theorists (among them Jacques Derrida) have argued that the signified is just as much a *signifier* (a word and not an image) as the signifier itself.

4. Peake, 15.

5. The *Oxford English Dictionary* has: "1638: Sanderson, *Serm.* II, 101. There is such a height and length and depth and breadth in that love; such a bathos in every dimension of it."

6. *Coleridge's Miscellaneous Criticism*, edited by T. M. Raynor (Cambridge: Cambridge University Press, 1936), 12.

7. Quoted in J. L. and Barbara Hammond, *Lord Shaftesbury* (Harmondsworth: Penguin, 1939), 258.

8. *The Works of Samuel Johnson*, IX; 16-17.

9. *Letters of Thomas Gray*, edited by Duncan Tovey (London: G. Bell, 1909), 2nd. ed., I; 44.

10. Russell, xii.

11. If one maintains that the verb "to feel" automatically involves an awareness of feeling, then the assertion that we can feel our superiority to an object of nature without being aware that we feel it, must be regarded as a contradiction in terms. One of the lessons of Kant's "Transcendental Aesthetic," however, is that sensation, perception and conception are distinct activities. While we cannot point to a particular moment at which the mind begins to "watch itself" (in Camus's phrase,) we can distinguish between states of mind on either side of that moment. In these terms, the hypothesis to be tested in the following examination of sublime texts is, that when the subject's capacities for irony and enthusiasm are simultaneously engaged, his mind rests, so to speak, on the cusp of that moment.

12. One thinks, among other examples, of the hero's reaction to the exhortation of St. Paul in Act II, scene vi of Hindemith's *Mathis der Maler*: "Geh hin und bilde!"; "Mich hat in dir Gott selbst berührt," etc. When signification is not a property of the medium (as in the case of pure music) it is easier to be sure that the sublime

emotion follows the storm (e.g. the soft passage [letters G through K, esp. bars 157-96] following the orchestral *tutti* [bars 139-43] in the first movement of Bruckner's *Eighth Symphony* [Vienna: Bruckner-Gesellschaft Verlag, 1972], 15-21).

13. Thorpe, 198.

14. Kant's emphasis is not on the negative function of comparison—on deriving a proof that "everything else" is inferior to the absolutely great—but on the "expansion of soul" which the subject sustains in the sublime moment. In other words, he emphasizes the positive side of the negative sublime, as here: "That which is sublime is said to be absolutely great. We must therefore distinguish it from magnitudes or definite quantities (*quanta*). The absolutely great is that which exceeds every definite quantity." ("Analytic of the Sublime," 94.)

15. Thorpe, 197.

16. John Ruskin coined this phrase in *Modern Painters*, vol. III (1856), ch. 12. It describes "the tendency of poets and painters to credit nature with the feelings of human beings." (J. K. Robinson, "Pathetic Fallacy," *Princeton Encyclopedia of Poetry and Poetics*, edited by A. Preminger [Princeton University Press, 1974].)

17. Quoted in Christopher Johnstone, *John Martin* (New York: St. Martin's Press, 1971), 16.

18. In a reference to the painting, the artist himself drew attention to this point: "Scale of proportion, a figure six feet high, by which the length of the halls is found to be one mile." (Quoted in Johnstone, 16.)

19. *Table Talk and Omniana of Samuel Taylor Coleridge*, 33-34.

20. Bradley, 41-45.

21. Ware, 60: "For Mrs. Radcliffe sublimity is a definite quantity and was indeed quantifiable."

22. Charles Robert Maturin, *Melmoth the Wanderer* (Lincoln: University of Nebraska Press, 1961), 22.

23. Sir Walter Scott, *Waverley* (London: Dent, 1906), 234.

24. Nicolson, 209.

25. John Ruskin, *The Stones of Venice* (London: Smith, Elder and Co., 1851-1853), vol. II, ch. 6.

Chapter Eleven

1. *The Works of Samuel Johnson*, IX; 16-17.

2. *Oeuvres complètes*, 384.

3. Richard, 57. This engagement bears particularly on the *topoi* of the *tombeau* and the *chevelure*.

4. *Oeuvres complètes*, 272.

5. Ibid., 502.

6. Quoted from *Anecdotes of Painting in England* (1771) in Mario Praz's "Introductory Essay" to *Three Gothic Novels*, edited by Peter Fairclough (Harmondsworth: Penguin, 1968), 16.

7. Donald Francis Tovey, *Essays in Musical Analysis* (London: Oxford University Press, 1972) III; 125.

8. Cf. Bernardin de Saint-Pierre: "nous avons encore en nous un sentiment plus sublime qui nous fait aimer les ruines . . ."; La Curne de Sainte-Palaye: "Jai gravi, mesuré les ruines sublimes . . ."; and Diderot: "O les belles, les sublimes ruines!" (quoted in Roland Mortier, *La Poétique des ruines en France* (Geneva: Droz, 1974), 93, 114, 129). Ruins appear to combine a suggestion of the "architecture une" (from which they are an obvious *déchéance*) with the "perspective on the temporal abyss" just mentioned: "[Elles] suggère[nt] . . . la petitesse de l'homme . . . le contraste saisissant entre la solidité de la matière et la fragilité humaine, et paradoxalement aussi leur contraire: le charme délicieux de l'instant conquis sur la fuite du temps" (Mortier, 92). Hence Diderot: "Il faut ruiner un palais pour en faire un objet d'intérêt." (Quoted in Mortier, 97.)

9. Quoted in Jean-Noël Pancrazi, *Mallarmé* (Paris: Hatier, 1973), 8.

10. *Oeuvres complètes*, 378.

11. This was the point of Coleridge's assertion that the "Llama's dung-pellet" might become the theme of a sublime discourse.

12. *Coleridge's Miscellaneous Criticism*, 164.

13. *Oeuvres complètes*, 565.

14. Gardner Davies defines this "tiers aspect" as follows: "[D'abord] le fait ou objet initial; puis cet objet, passant en son aspect contraire ou négatif, s'abolit et ne laisse subsister qu'une réminiscence abstraite. Finalement, cette réminiscence et l'absence effective de l'objet matériel se concilient en une troisième conception, qui est la 'notion idéale.' " *Vers une explication rationnelle du "Coup de dés"* (Paris: Corti, 1953), 46.

15. *Oeuvres complètes*, 366. Why should the functions of *reportage* and *allumage* be incompatible? "Un désir indéniable à mon temps est de séparer *comme en vue d'attributions différentes* le double état de la parole, brut ou immédiat ici, là essentiel" (*Oeuvres complètes*, p. 857, italics added). It is possible that in the projected "Grand Oeuvre" (*Oeuvres complètes*, p. 662) the two functions were both to be accomplished: for if the "explication de la terre" were to be truly comprehensive, would not the "état brut, l'état de moindre développement" of language have to be represented as well? (Backès, p. 36.) So long, however, as the poet confined himself to "études en vue de mieux" (*Oeuvres complètes*, p. 77) his aim was to write in a fashion as little contingent on the *actual* as possible.

16. *Oeuvres complètes*, 366. The refusal was of course theoretical rather than practical: even "la notion pure" must be set down in black and white.

17. Kristeva, 19.

18. *Oeuvres complètes*, 385. This analogy is implicit in Mallarmé's references to his "patience d'alchimiste" and to his preparation for "l'Oeuvre, le Grand Oeuvre, comme disaient les alchimistes, nos ancêtres" (*Oeuvres complètes*, 662). Apparently he conceived the "tiers aspect" of language to be analogous to the quintessence of matter. Note also his use of the verb *sublimiter* in the passage discussed in chapter twelve, section IV.

19. *Oeuvres complètes*, 455, 381.

20. Longinus, 107.

21. *Oeuvres complètes*, 869.

22. Ibid., 883.

23. Ibid., 384.

24. Lehmann, p. 92n. Cf. *Oeuvres complètes*, 257: "Toute chose sacrée et qui veut demeurer sacrée s'enveloppe de mystère."

25. *Oeuvres complètes*, 56.

26. *Correspondance I: 1862–1871*, 207.

27. "Ce à quoi nous devons viser surtout est que, dans le poème, les mots . . . se reflètent les uns sur les autres jusqu'à paraître ne plus avoir leur couleur propre, mais n'être que les transitions d'une gamme." (Letter to Coppée, 5 December 1866.) "Le sens . . . est evoqué par un mirage interne des mots mêmes." (Letter to Cazalis, 18 July 1868.)

28. Weiskel, 11.

29. Jean Starobinski, "Mallarmé et la tradition poétique française," *Les Lettres* 3, special number on Mallarmé (1948), 43.

30. Letter to Cazalis, 14 May 1867.

31. The import of this negative metaphor was discussed in chapter five.

32. *Oeuvres complètes*, 364.

33. Ibid., 67.

34. *Correspondance I: 1862–1871*, 207.

35. *Oeuvres complètes*, 654. While it is true that an instinct requires no objective justification to operate in a particular case, it is also true that where such a justification is lacking, the instinct has no object to accomplish or goal to attain. Thus the "instinct de ciel" is a delusion because unless *le ciel* is regarded as a metonym for the Being who implanted the instinct in the subject, it can have no a priori attraction for the latter.

36. This incident is described in Charles Chassé, *Les Clefs de Mallarmé* (Paris: Aubier, 1954), 19.

37. *Oeuvres complètes*, 389.

38. Jean-Louis Backès has noticed "la contradiction que recèle [ce] titre . . .: 'allégorie' veut dire 'parole à propos d'autre chose.' Comment l'autre peut-il être lui-même?" *Poésies de Mallarmé* (Paris: Hachette, 1973), 24.

39. *Oeuvres complètes*, 663. The idea that all potential effects of a text but those desired by the author can be eliminated by a dispassionate approach to composition, was voiced by Mallarmé in the remarks discussed in chapter twelve, section VI. It was earlier advanced by Poe in "The Poetic Principle."

40. "More" and "least" refer here to the parameters of a relative condition.

41. *Oeuvres complètes*, 565.

42. Ibid., 370.

43. Letter to Aubanel, 16 July 1866.

44. *Oeuvres complètes*, 500.

45. E. M. Forster, "Joseph Conrad: A Note," *Abinger Harvest* (New York: Harcourt, Brace & Co., 1936), 138.

46. *Oeuvres complètes*, 55. Mysticism is employed in its broadest sense here as a rubric for all the statements in which Mallarmé suggested that it is possible to attain the absolute through art. The following remarks of Weiskel's are pertinent in the context of our observations respecting the impossibility of producing the sublime experience by enthusiasm alone: "For the judgment of the sublime comes into play precisely insofar as man cannot attain the totality; the intensity of the sublime experience is a direct function of the impossibility of realizing (in any way) . . . any supersensible idea" (p. 45). And "insofar as there is an insistence upon realizing man's infinitude imaginatively (as in Blake) or materially (as in idealist utopianism), the sublime moment must disappear" (p. 44).

47. René Nelli, " 'Igitur' ou l'argument ontologique retourné," *Les Lettres* 3, special number on Mallarmé (1948), 147.

48. E.g. by Edith and Richard Sterba, *Beethoven and His Nephew: A Psychoanalytic Study of Their Relationship* (New York: Schocken, 1971), 93.

49. *Oeuvres complètes*, 399 (italics added).

50. Georges Poulet, "Mallarmé," *Etudes sur le temps humain II: la distance intérieure* (Paris: Plon, 1952), 337.

51. *Oeuvres complètes*, 295, 384.

52. Ibid., 381.

53. This was Kant's term for the movement of mind that disposes one mistakenly to regard an object of nature as an embodiment of the absolute; thus one substitutes "a respect (*Achtung*) for the Object in place of one for the idea of humanity in our own self—the Subject." ("Analytic of the Sublime," 106.)

54. The "individuating difference" is described in Duns Scotus, *Philosophical Writings*, translated and edited by Allan Wolter (Edinburgh: Nelson, 1962), 166.

55. "Analytic of the Sublime," 121.

56. "Normal" insofar as the subject's desire should be directed at objects external to himself.

57. *Oeuvres complètes*, 58.

58. Ibid., 66, 68, 74, 368.

59. Edward Caird, *A Critical Account of the Philosophy of Kant* (Glasgow: Maclehose, 1877), 608.

60. Or to put the matter more plainly, agnostic tenets imply that any claim to have realized the ideal in language is invalid; yet agnosticism cannot account for the intimation of the ideal that sublime discourse affords.

61. Gérard Genette, "Bonheur de Mallarmé?" *Tel Quel* 10 (1962), 62.

62. *Oeuvres complètes*, 865.

Chapter Twelve

1. This order is determined by the fidelity and completeness with which the content of the passages confirms the model of the sublime proposed in part one.

2. Littré defines the *style sublime* as a "Style dont la grandeur vient de celle des pensées, que la simplicité de l'expression fait surtout ressortir" (*Dictionnaire de la langue française*, 4; 2057). Cf. *Grand Larousse de la langue française*, 6; 5767: "Style propre aux genres les plus élevés . . . comme la tragédie."

3. Chapter twelve, section III.

4. Unlike the connotation of etheriality which it contributed to the metaphor of sublimation quoted earlier, *le gaz* appears here to emphasize (through its *sème* of utility) the *reality* of the "lumière," and hence to reinforce the pejorative tone of the sentence as a whole. Cf. "Le Tombeau de Charles Baudelaire": "Ou que le gaz récent torde la mèche *louche" (Oeuvres complètes*, 70, italics added.)

5. For this reason it seems logical to regard "femme" as a positive contrast to "bête" in this context. Since the "femme" is not an object, but a metaphor for the subject here, the general truth of Starobinski's remark does not apply: "Au départ la thématique de Mallarmé se distingue mal de la thématique baudelairienne. Ce "néant" qu'il devait plus tard décanter jusqu'au plus haut degré d'anonymat, il lui a donné pendant longtemps le masque charnel de la femme et de la prostitution." ("Mallarmé et la tradition poétique française," 43.)

6. The second formulation defines the poet's office more precisely than the first: he is allowed the stewardship, not the proprietorship, of the treasure of rhythm, which properly belongs, as the adjective "antérieur" makes clear, to the "répertoire éternel de l'Idéal."

7. "Adjuvant" from the Latin *juvare, to help*. Gautier's poetry is the temporal means by which the subject is helped to the experience of the ideal.

8. This accumulation also served the function of hyperbole by emphasizing the distance between the admirer and the admired object.

9. The dedication of *Les Fleurs du mal* to Gautier begins: "AU POETE IMPECCABLE, AU PARFAIT MAGICIEN ES LETTRES FRANÇAISES."

10. (Italics added.) Of his two interpretations, the first is more plausible than the second. He can suggest that the tear is an expression of animal pleasure ("volupté")—albeit of a pleasure so rarified that the drop it elicits from him is not cloudy but transparent—without entering into a comparison. But to assign a divine provenance within his body to the drop, and convert it, as though by a process of sublimation, into a "parfum," he must employ the word "comme," and introduce the idea of difference.

11. For a longer discussion of the symbolism of tears see Marvick, "Stendhal's *Armance*: Speech and Silence" (unpublished Master's thesis, Columbia University, 1976), 47–50.

12. This is an emendation of the more straightforward version given on p. 1546 of the *Oeuvres complètes.*

13. Both verbs derive from the Latin *tangere, to touch.*

14. Mallarmé does, however, use the verb *toucher* in the sense of *to attaint* in his Oxford lecture on "La Musique et les lettres." The vogue for free verse is deplored in the passage beginning: "On a touché au vers." (*Oeuvres complètes,* 643.)

15. The text tells us that the Poet could understand them; but Nature waits until he is gone. The argument of the paragraph is announced in the first three words, "Loin de tout." It describes the impossibility of knowing what Kant called the "thing in itself."

16. This is only one explanation of the phrase. The rite may be vain because it produces no result; or because it is excessively "splendid." Cf. the pejorative use of "splendides" in chapter twelve, section I.

17. Mallarmé's indebtedness to Littré is persuasively if cantankerously argued by Chassé, 36–42.

18. One also notices the duplication of the verb "piquer" in Littré's etymology of *prestige* ("ce qui pique . . . d'avance) and in his definition of the verb *poindre*, which Mallarmé used of Hamlet in the phrase "étranger à tous lieux où il poind" (302).

19. Charles Lamb, "On the Tragedies of Shakespeare" (1811), reprinted in *Four Centuries of Shakespearean Criticism*, edited by Frank Kermode (New York: Avon, 1965), 356–66.

20. Mallarmé refers to his "presque nudité sombre" (300).

21. "Dans l'idéale peinture de la scène tout se meut *selon une réciprocité symbolique des types entre eux ou relativement à une figure seule*" (301).

22. Pancrazi, 8: "Aussi n'est-il pas question pour Mallarmé de rivaliser avec la nature, en prétendant se livrer à une quelconque 'création.' "

23. That is, it affords the subject a sense of his connection with the absolute by undoing the subreption of the object (here, the spectacle).

24. That the entire passage refers to Banville appears as a confirmation of Mallarmé's argument. Cf. Baudelaire, referring to the word *lyre*, that occurs with significant frequency in Banville's verse: "La *lyre* exprime en effet cet état presque surnaturel, cette intensité de vie où l'âme *chante*, où elle est *contrainte* de chanter, comme l'arbre, l'oiseau et la mer." ("Théodore de Banville," *Oeuvres complètes*, 735–36, italics in original); and Mallarmé, *Oeuvres complètes*, 264: "Banville, qui n'est pas un homme, mais la voix même de la lyre."

25. *Oeuvres complètes*, 262. This declaration immediately preceded the passage from the "Symphonie littéraire" discussed above.

26. The metaphor of dialectic for the structure of rhymed verse has obvious limitations. The process of systematic inquiry by which the relative truth of a proposition is determined, for example, has no counterpart in the merely formal necessity of inventing a second verse to rhyme with, and complete, the first. And whereas

dialectic is self-perpetuating (each synthesis becoming in turn the thesis of a new debate), the alexandrine is not: every couplet must begin *ex nihilo*. Dialectic, however, has been invoked before now in connection with Mallarmé's imagery: the setting sun, for instance, "forme l'un des instants-charnière d'une dialectique concrète de l'être et du non-être" (Richard, 156).

27. For example, "Le domaine publique, où un laps révolu de cinquante ans précipite la propriété des ouvrages de l'esprit, en désaccord avec l'hérédité vulgaire" (*Oeuvres complètes*, 638); "[mes] contemporains ne savent pas lire—"(*Oeuvres complètes*, 386). Cf. *Correspondance I*, 93, 168; *Correspondance II*, 76, 100-101; *Correspondance III*, 227. Paula Lewis in *The Aesthetics of Stéphane Mallarmé in Relation to His Public* (Cranbury: Associated University Presses, 1976) opines that his "calm aristocratic scorn . . . existed only on the surface," and adds that "in his maturity Mallarmé did exhibit a strong desire to effect [a] reconciliation between himself and society" (216). See also Paul Bénichou, "Mallarmé et le public," *L'Ecrivain et ses travaux* (Paris: Corti, 1967), 69-88; and Marshall McLuhan, "Joyce, Mallarmé, and the Press," *The Sewanee Review* 62; 1 (January-March 1954), 38-55.

28. Here again the term is used of one who expects to "realize man's infinitude either imaginatively . . . or materially."

29. Cf. the "moderne émersion" of "eternal" Poetry from Gautier's brain as described in section II of this chapter.

30. Quoted in Pancrazi, 16.

31. This sympathy is described in Holbrook Jackson, *The Eighteen-Nineties* (New York: G. P. Putnam's Sons, 1966), 94, 100, 274.

32. There is, however, a tradition (originating with the Babylonian Gnostic Mani, 216-277 A.D.) that regards the dark not merely as the absence of light but as a principle of absolute importance in itself. Mallarmé's presentation of the void as the indispensible adjunct of the stars in the passage discussed immediately below, suggests that our statement concerning superlatives should be qualified, so far as it refers to his writings, as a statement concerning positive superlatives.

33. Cf. *Correspondance I: 1862–1871*, 246: "Je n'ai crée mon oeuvre que par *élimination*"; and Joseph Conrad, referring to the "art of the novelist": "Every success is resumed in the supreme energy of an act of renunciation." (*Notes of Life and Letters* [London: Dent, 1921], 16.)

34. *Oeuvres complètes*, 522.

35. Ibid., 870.

36. Ibid., 379 (italics added).

37. *Paradise Lost*, Book I, line 62.

38. *Oeuvres complètes*, 370.

39. The *Oxford English Dictionary*'s fourth definition of "ideal" reads: "Existing only in idea; confined to thought or imagination . . . opp. to *real or actual*." Cf. Littrés first definition: "Qui n'a pas d'existence que dans l'idée, dans l'esprit; . . . chimérique."

40. This is the more true in that the text is subtitled "Conférence." The words "rien existe" could have been pronounced with the liaison, so as to be aurally indistinguishable from the words "rien n'existe."

41. The absolute pretensions of the poet are revealed in his admitted desire to contribute to the "répertoire éternel de l'Idéal" (*Oeuvres complètes*, 262). Those of the objective world, however, must be understood as projections of the subject. The question is not whether the objective world nourishes a pretension, but whether the subject regards it as his rival (for the favor of the absolute) and imputes a pretension to it.

42. Davies, 164–65 (italics added).

43. The concentrated language of this passage may require some elucidation. The "voile" and the "mousselines de l'Inde" are metaphors for the sublime language of the eighteenth-century Oriental tale. Since that language was merely the cover for what Mallarmé considered the unliterary purposes of instruction or edification ("abstractions politiques ou morales") it is said to result

in the creation of travesties. The scientific efforts of Mallarmé's contemporaries to evoke the ancient world have failed (with some exceptions) to bridge the gulf of intervening years. They have failed to produce an eternally durable synthesis that would discharge reliably ("tonner") upon every rereading; that would never become "hors de mode." The images of the *éclair* and the stars at noon, then, are metaphors for the intellectual and imaginative effect of reading a successful treatment of the past—an "idéal mêlant époques et races."

44. *Oeuvres complètes*, 376.

45. That Mallarmé regarded poetry as a craft is attested by his definition of the poet as a "penseur sérieux" whose works are "lentement ciselées"; and by his celebration of the "gloire ardente du métier" (*Oeuvres complètes*, 54).

46. The association of rhythm with the act of passing beyond is also made in Baudelaire's prose-poem "Le Thyrse": "Cher Liszt, à travers les brumes, par delà les fleuves, par-dessus les villes, où les pianos chantent votre gloire" (*Oeuvres complètes*, 285).

47. Cf. *Oeuvres complètes*, 372: "il n'est pas de Présent, non—un présent n'existe pas."

48. This transposition of the final images of the passage into our own critical metalanguage is clearly sanctioned by their explicit presentation in the text as metaphors for the intellectual effect of reading a successful prose treatment of the past. It is not we, but Mallarmé, who presents the images as descriptions of the activity of reading. The *éclair de l'Orient* has nowhere to discharge but in the reader's mind.

49. The adjective is ambiguously placed. Its microcontext (and the claims to legendary origin of Beckford's tale) seem to attach it to "l'Orient"; but the image as a whole anticipates the "évanouissement" of the peri's wing in the final sentence, and as such makes more sense when read as a description of the moment after the flash of lightning. Alternatively one might regard *l'éclair de l'Orient* as a compound noun and argue that the adjective modifies *Orient* as well as its metonym *éclair*.

50. *Oeuvres complètes*, 857.

51. Michael Riffaterre, "On Deciphering Mallarmé," 85-87; and in chapter five.

52. *Oeuvres complètes*, 367.

53. Ibid., 869. The presence of the verb *croire* in this description casts an appreciable doubt on the reality of the reader's recreative function. This doubt, however, is fully consistent with our own argument concerning the power of enthusiasm to distort the perception of "reality and truth"—for as was noted earlier, Mallarmé believed that "c'est le lecteur qui doit être inspiré," whereas "l'enthousiasme n'est pas un état d'âme d'écrivain."

54. The image, in other words, is to be regarded as "evidence sufficing to establish a fact" (*Oxford English Dictionary*). The fact, here, is the cause that must be postulated to account for the occurrence of the actions represented by the image, as well as for any qualitative peculiarities in the image that cannot be explained by any other possible cause.

55. This image has two distinct literary antecedents, both of interest in relation to the concept of the sublime. The theme of the stars being visible at noon from the summit of a mountain or at the bottom of a well may be regarded as a variation on the imagery of extreme height and depth that was a constant feature of the natural sublime. Also, a figurative description of the enthusiastic state of mind in which the subject believes in the ideality of an object of perception, is found in the phrase "faire voir à quelqu'un les étoiles à midi," which Littré paraphrases as "lui en imposer, lui en faire accroire" (*Dictionnaire de la langue française*, 6; 5767).

56. Mallarmé elsewhere associates *le midi* with a single, omnipotent presence: "L'or frappe, maintenant, d'aplomb la race . . . il décrit sa trajectoire vers l'omnipotence—éclat, l'unique, attardé pour un midi imperturbable" (*Oeuvres complètes*, 410).

Chapter Thirteen

1. *Oeuvres complètes*, 867.

2. This quality was even more pronounced in the image, recalling that of a *feu d'artifice,* quoted earlier. The function of enthusiasm, as we showed in chapters seven and eight, is to suspend the subject's capacity to distinguish the relative value or importance of objects (or representations). Those distinctions require that the subject's capacity for ironic perception be engaged.

3. Here and in the foregoing analysis of the image of the stars at noon we have based our argument on Kant's distinction between the categories of reason and imagination, and on his attribution of the idea of the absolute (which is a "noumenon") to the former.

4. J. Charpentier, *L'Evolution de la poésie lyrique: De J. Delorme à P. Claudel* (Paris: Les Oeuvres representatives, 1931), 126.

5. Richard, 45.

6. Emilie Noulet, *L'Oeuvre poétique de Stéphane Mallarmé,* rev. ed. (Brussels: Editions Jacques Antoine, 1974), 68.

7. Ibid., 67.

8. Lines 1, 5 and 6. The irony of the ideal (*l'azur*) lies in the fact that it is at once near to us (as the concretizing attribution of the *regard* makes clear) and unattainable (as the impossibility of retaining its blueness in any limited quantity suggests).

9. Weiskel, 29.

10. The diagnosis is of course not medical but figurative. The similarity disorder is invoked here to describe a condition analogous to that of the speaker at the end of "L'Azur," whose reiteration of the same noun four times suggests an impairment of the associative faculty that would enable him to develop his poem by metaphorical substitution.

11. A successful outcome of the same attempt was recounted in the prose poem discussed in chapter twelve, section II.

12. Those, in other words, in which the subject's recognition of the unattainability of the ideal is counteracted by a lively respect for the objects of signification. Such respect (as the following partial list of sublime poems suggests) tends to express itself in an affirmative or

celebratory use of language; in a willingness to name things rather than to avoid naming them.

13. Richard, 182.

14. While the tense of the verb denotes a missed opportunity, it nonetheless affirms that the opportunity to be born did exist at some time. Thus the defeat of hope is mitigated by the consolation of regret.

15. Richard, 183.

16. Ibid., 247.

17. Ibid.

18. Gans, "Prose poétique," 190, 193.

19. Richard, 174.

20. The lines quoted below partially substantiate this point. Note also her attachment to her "froides pierreries"; her assertion that the nurse's attempt to touch her "refroidit mon sang"; her claim to sisterhood with the star "qui brûle de chasteté"; and her desire to depart for the land where "Vénus . . . brûle dans le feuillage."

21. Longinus, 114 (italics added).

22. Richard, 174 (italics in original).

23. Eric Gans, "Pornographie et délire," *Poésie* 6 (1978), 115.

Conclusion

1. Kenneth Clark, *The Gothic Revival: An Essay in the History of Taste* (New York: Harper and Row, 1974), 42.

2. We interpreted this emphasis on the terror inspired by natural spectacles as an attempt to restore to God the claim to absolute awe and respect (in Kant's sense of the term) which he had forfeited by "marrying the world of appearances." That claim remained absolute, we argued, only so long as He did.

3. "Analytic of the Sublime," 108.

4. As late as 1846 these were still to be met with. The hurricane described in chapter four of G. W. M. Reynolds's *Faust* (London: G. Vickers), causes "huge masses of granite" to be "hurled down into the abysses beneath," where "they threw up the spray to a tremendous height, as if a volcano had exploded in the caverns of the earth and heaved up the bed of the torrents" (45–46).

5. To these may be added "his other 'masks' of the poet: Igitur, the Faun, . . . Poe . . . [and] the *stature mignonne ténébreuse debout* . . . in *Un Coup de dés*." R. G. Cohn, *Toward the Poems of Mallarmé* (Berkeley: University of California Press, 1980), 52, 86.

6. Perhaps the inherent impossibility of this attempt explains why Mallarmé regarded writing as a "jeu *insensé*."

7. *Critique of Practical Reason*, translated and edited by Lewis W. Beck (Chicago: University of Chicago Press, 1949), 232: "Therefore morals is not really the doctrine of how to make ourselves happy but of how we are to be worthy of happiness."

Selected Bibliography

Abastado, Claude. *Expérience et théorie de la création poétique chez Mallarmé. Archives des lettres modernes*, 4; 119, 1970.

Abrams, M. H. *The Mirror and the Lamp: Romantic Theory and the Critical Tradition.* London: Oxford University Press, 1953.

Addison, Joseph. "On the Pleasures of the Imagination." *The Spectator*, no. 412 (23 June 1712).

———. *Remarks on Several Parts of Italy.* London: J. Tonson, 1705.

Albrecht, W. P. *The Sublime Pleasures of Tragedy.* Lawrence: University of Kansas Press, 1975.

Alison, Archibald. *Essays on the Nature and Principles of Taste.* Edinburgh: Bell and Bradfute, 1790.

Backès, Jean-Louis. *Poésies de Mallarmé.* Paris: Hachette, 1973.

Blake, William. "Annotations to Reynolds's *Discourses,*" *Complete Writings.* Edited by Geoffrey Keynes. Oxford: Oxford University Press, 1972.

Boileau-Despréaux, Nicholas. *Traité du Sublime.* Translation of Longinus, *Peri Hupsous. Oeuvres completes,* vol. III. Edited by A. C. Gidel. Paris: Garnier, 1871-1873.

Boulay, Daniel. *L'Obscurité esthétique de Mallarmé et la "Prose pour des Esseintes"*. Paris: D. Boulay, 1960.

Bradley, A. C. "The Sublime". *Oxford Lectures on Poetry.* London: Macmillan, 1909, 37-68.

Brody, Jules. *Boileau and Longinus.* Geneva: Droz, 1958.

Burke, Edmund. *A Philosophical Inquiry into the Origin of Our Ideas of the Sublime and Beautiful. The Works of the Right Honorable Edmund Burke.* 4th edition, vol I. Boston: Little, Brown, 1871.

Caird, Edward. *A Critical Account of the Philosophy of Kant.* Glasgow: Maclehose, 1877.

Charpentier, J. *L'Evolution de la poésie lyrique: De J. Delorme à P. Claudel.* Paris: Les Oeuvres représentatives, 1931.

Chassé, Charles. *Les Clefs de Mallarmé.* Paris: Aubier, 1954.

Chisholm, A. R. *Mallarmé's "Grand Oeuvre."* Manchester: Manchester University Press, 1962.

Clark, Kenneth. *The Gothic Revival: An Essay in the History of Taste.* New York: Harper and Row, 1974.

Cohn, Robert Greer. *Toward the Poems of Mallarmé.* Berkeley: University of California Press, 1980.

Coleridge, Samuel Taylor. *Coleridge's Miscellaneous Criticism.* Edited by T. M. Raynor. Cambridge: Cambridge University Press, 1936.

———. *The Complete Works of Samuel Taylor Coleridge,* vol. II. Edited by W. G. Shedd. New York: Harper, 1864.

———. *Letters of Samuel Taylor Coleridge.* Edited by E. H. Coleridge. London: Heinemann, 1895.

———. *The Table Talk and Omniana of Samuel Taylor Coleridge.* Edited by T. Ashe. London: G. Bell, 1903.

———. *Unpublished Letters of Samuel Taylor Coleridge,* 2 vols. Edited by E. L. Griggs. New Haven: Yale University Press, 1933.

Conrad, Joseph. *Notes on Life and Letters.* London: Dent, 1921.

Crane, Ronald S. Review of Monk, *The Sublime. Philological Quarterly* XV; ii (April 1936), 166-67.

Croce, Benedetto. *Aesthetic as Science of Expression and General Linguistic.* 2nd. ed. Translated by Douglass Ainslee. London: Macmillan, 1929.

Cuénot, Claude. "L'Origine des *Contes indiens.*" *Mercure de France* 288 (15 November 1938), 117-26.

Davies, Gardner. *Vers une explication rationnelle du "Coup de dés."* Paris: Corti, 1953.

Dennis, John. *The Advancement and Reformation of Modern Poetry, a Critical Discourse.* London: R. Parker, 1701.

———. *The Critical Works of John Dennis,* vol I. Edited by E. N. Hooker. Baltimore: The Johns Hopkins Press, 1939.

———. *The Grounds of Criticism in Poetry. The Select Works of Mr. John Dennis,* vol. II. London: J. Darby, 1718.

De Gourmont, Remy. "Stéphane Mallarmé." *Selected Writings.* Edited and translated by Glenn Burne. Ann Arbor: University of Michigan Press, 1966.

De Quincey, Thomas. "Milton." *Biographical and Historical Essays.* Boston: Houghton, 1880, 118-34.

Eliot, T. S. "Christopher Marlowe." *Essays on Elizabethan Drama.* New York: Harcourt, Brace, Jovanovitch, 1960, 56-64.

———. "Note sur Mallarmé et Poe." *Nouvelle Revue Française* xi (1926), 525.

Ellis, Havelock. *Selected Essays.* London: Dent, 1966.

Emerson, Ralph Waldo. *The Journals and Notebooks of Ralph Waldo Emerson,* vol. VII. Edited by A. W. Plumstead. Cambridge: Harvard University Press, 1969.

Ende, Stuart. *Keats and the Sublime.* New Haven: Yale University Press, 1976.

Fontanier, Pierre. *Les Figures du discours.* Paris: Flammarion, 1968.

Gans, Eric L. "Hyperbole et ironie." *Littérature* 24 (1975), 488-94.

———. "Pornographie et délire." *Poésie* 6 (1978), 110-25.

———. "Prose poétique." *Romanic Review* 66; 3 (1975), 187-98.

Genette, Gérard. "Bonheur de Mallarmé?" *Tel Quel* 10 (1962), 61-65.

Gray, Thomas. *Letters of Thomas Gray.* Edited by Duncan Tovey. London: G. Bell, 1909.

Hagstrum, Jean H. *Samuel Johnson's Literary Criticism.* Chicago: University of Chicago Press, 1952.

Hazlitt, William. "The Character of Milton's Satan"; "Sir Thomas Browne." *William Hazlitt, Essayist and Critic: Selections from His Writings.* Edited by A. Ireland. London: Wayne, 1889.

———. "On Shakespeare's Comedy." *Four Centuries of Shakespearean Criticism.* Edited by Frank Kermode. New York: Avon, 1965, 221-30.

Henn, Thomas Rice. *Longinus and English Criticism.* Cambridge: Cambridge University Press, 1934.

Hipple, Walter. *The Beautiful, the Sublime and the Pathetic in Eighteenth-Century British Aesthetic Theory.* Cambridge: Cambridge University Press, 1957.

Hopkins, Gerard Manley. *Poems and Prose.* Edited by W. H. Gardner. Harmondsworth: Penguin, 1963.

Hussey, Christopher. *The Picturesque: Studies in a Point of View.* London and New York: G. Putnam's Sons, 1927.

Irwin, Michael, "Wordsworth's 'Dependency Sublime.' " *Essays in Criticism* 14; 4 (October 1964), 352-62.

Jackson, Holbrook. *The Eighteen-Nineties.* New York: G. P. Putnam's Sons, 1966.

Jakobson, Roman, and Morris Halle. "Two Aspects of Language and Two Types of Aphasic Disturbances." *Fundamentals of Language.* The Hague: Mouton, 1956, 55-82.

Jankélévitch, Vladimir. *L'Ironie.* Paris: Flammarion, 1964.

Johnson, Samuel. *Rambler*, no 137. *The Works of Samuel Johnson*, vol. III. Oxford: Oxford University Press, 1825.

———. *Lives of the English Poets.* 3 vols. Edited by G. B. Hill. Oxford: Oxford University Press, 1907.

Johnstone, Christopher. *John Martin.* New York: St. Martin's Press, 1971.

Kant, Immanuel. "Analytic of the Sublime." *The Critique of Judgment.* Translated by J. C. Meredith. Oxford: Oxford University Press, 1969, 90-204.

———. *Observations on the Feeling of the Beautiful and the Sublime.* Translated by John T. Goldthwait. Berkeley: University of California Press, 1960.

Keats, John. *Letters of John Keats.* Edited by M. B. Forman. Oxford: Oxford University Press, 1935.

Kristeva, Julia. *Pouvoirs de l'horreur: essai sur l'abjection.* Paris: Seuil, 1980.

Lehmann, A. G. *The Symbolist Aesthetic in France: 1885-1895.* Oxford: Basil Blackwell, 1968.

Lewis, Clive Staples. *Selected Literary Essays.* Edited by Walter Hooper. Cambridge: Cambridge University Press, 1979.

Lewis, Paula Gilbert. *The Aesthetics of Stéphane Mallarmé in Relation to His Public.* Cranbury: Associated University Presses, 1976.

Litman, Théodore A. *Le Sublime en France: 1660–1714.* Paris: Nizet, 1971.

Longinus. *On the Sublime. Classical Literary Criticism.* Edited and translated by T. S. Dorsch. Harmondsworth: Penguin, 1965.

———. *On the Sublime.* Edited and translated by D. A. Russell. Oxford: Oxford University Press, 1965.

Mallarmé, Stéphane. *Correspondance I: 1862–1871, II: 1871–1885, III: 1886–1889.* Edited by Henri Mondor and Lloyd James Austin. Paris: NRF Gallimard, 1959, 1965, 1969.

———. *Oeuvres complètes.* Edited by Henri Mondor and G. Jean-Aubry. Paris: Gallimard "Bibliothèque de la Pléiade," 1945.

———. *Propos sur la poésie.* Edited by Henri Mondor. Monaco: Editions du Rocher, 1953.

Mauron, Charles. *Mallarmé l'obscur.* Paris: Corti, 1968.

Mill, John Stuart. "Thoughts on Poetry and Its Varieties." *Dissertations and Discussions: Political, Philosophical, and Historical.* London: J. W. Parker, 1859, 51–76.

———. *Three Essays on Religion.* London: Longmans, 1923.

Monk, Samuel H. *The Sublime: A Study of Critical Theories in XVIII-Century England.* New York: Modern Language Association of America, 1935.

Morris, David B. *The Religious Sublime.* Lexington: University of Kentucky Press, 1972.

Nelli, René. " 'Igitur' ou l'argument ontologique retourné." *Les Lettres,* 3, numéro spécial (1948), 147–54.

Nicolson, Marjorie. *Mountain Gloom and Mountain Glory: The Development of the Aesthetics of the Infinite.* New York: Norton, 1959.

Noulet, Emilie. *L'Oeuvre poétique de Stéphane Mallarmé.* Rev. edition. Brussels: Jacques Antoine, 1974.

———. *Vingt poèmes de Stéphane Mallarmé.* Geneva: Droz, 1967.

Pancrazi, Jean-Noël. *Mallarmé.* Paris: Hatier, 1973.

Paxton, Norman. *The Development of Mallarmé's Prose Style.* Geneva: Droz, 1968.

Peake, Charles. *Poetry of the Landscape and the Night: Two Eighteenth-Century Traditions.* Columbia: University of South Carolina Press, 1967.

Poe, Edgar Allan. "The Poetic Principle." *Representative Selections.* Edited by M. Alterton. New York: American Book Co., 1935.

Pope, Alexander. "An Essay on Criticism." *Poetical Works.* Edited by Herbert Davy. Oxford: Oxford University Press, 1966.

Poulet, Georges. "Mallarmé." *Etudes sur le temps humain II: la distance intérieure.* Paris: Plon, 1952, 298-355.

Raymond, Marcel. *De Baudelaire au surréalisme.* Rev. ed. Paris: Corti, 1966.

Riffaterre, Michael. "On Deciphering Mallarmé." *The Georgia Review* 29; 1 (1975), 75-91.

Ruskin, John. *The Stones of Venice.* London: Smith, Elder and Co., 1851-1853.

———. *Modern Painters,* vols. I and III. New York: J. Wiley, 1856, 1872.

Saussure, Ferdinand. *Cours de linguistique générale.* 3rd ed. Paris: Payot, 1967.

Schérer, Jacques. *L'Expression littéraire dans l'oeuvre de Mallarmé.* Paris: Nizet, 1947.

———. *Grammaire de Mallarmé.* Paris: Nizet, 1977.

Shelley, Percy B. "A Defence of Poetry." *Shelley's Literary and Philosophical Criticism.* Edited by J. Shawcross. London: H. Milford, 1909.

Sikes, Herschel M. "The Poetic Theory and Practice of Keats: The Record of a Debt to Hazlitt." *Philological Quarterly* 38; 4 (October 1954).

Soula, Camille. *Gloses sur Mallarmé.* Paris: Diderot, 1945.

Starobinski, Jean. "Mallarmé et la tradition poétique française." *Les Lettres,* 3 numéro spécial (1948), 35-45.

Stover, Frederick. " 'Sublime' as Applied to Nature." *Modern Language Notes* 70; 7 (November 1955), 484-87.

Swinburne, Algernon Charles. "Christopher Marlowe." *Swinburne as Critic.* Edited by Clyde K. Hyder. London: Routledge, 1972, 278-85.

Thorpe, Clarence DeWitt. "Coleridge on the Sublime." *Wordsworth and Coleridge: Studies in Honor of George McLean Harper.* Edited by Earl L. Griggs. Princeton: Princeton University Press, 1939.

Tuveson, Ernest. "Space, Deity and the 'Natural' Sublime." *Modern Language Quarterly* 12 (1951), 20-38.

Ware, Malcolm. *Sublimity in the Novels of Ann Radcliffe.* Upsala: English Institute, 1963.

Weiskel, Thomas. *The Romantic Sublime: Studies in the Structure and Psychology of Transcendence.* Baltimore: Johns Hopkins University Press, 1976.

Whalley, George. "Sublime." *Princeton Encyclopedia of Poetry and Poetics.* Edited by A. Preminger. Princeton: Princeton University Press, 1974.

Wood, Theodore. *The Word 'Sublime' and Its Context: 1650–1700.* The Hague: Mouton, 1972.

Wordsworth, William. *Letters of the Wordsworth Family from 1787 to 1855.* Edited by William Knight. Boston and London: Ginn and Co. 1907.

Index of Proper Names